*Fragile Hope*

# Thomas G. Bandy

# Fragile Hope

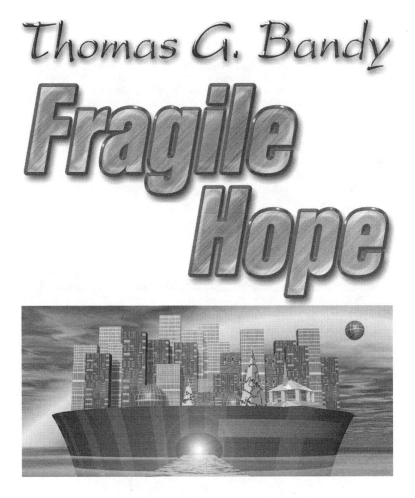

## Your Church In 2020

Abingdon Press
*Nashville*

**FRAGILE HOPE**

*Copyright © 2002 by Abingdon Press*

*This book is printed on recycled, acid-free paper.*

Library of Congress Cataloging-in-Publication Data

Bandy, Thomas G., 1950-
    Fragile hope / Thomas G. Bandy.
        p. cm.
    ISBN 0-687-02708-X (pbk. : alk. paper)
    1. Church renewal. I. Title.
BV600.3 .B365 2002
262'.001'7—dc21

2002010555

02 03 04 05 06 07 08 09 10 11—10 9 8 7 6 5 4 3 2 1

MANUFACTURED IN THE UNITED STATES OF AMERICA

*To all those Canadian and American clergy and lay leaders,*

*courageously struggling to lead their churches*

*to pursue an ancient Christian mission*

*in contemporary pagan times*

# CONTENTS

# One

# THE QUO VADIS MOMENT

The transformational story of Peter is the precarious promise to the Christian church in our time. His story is that of a traditional participant in organized religion who is chosen, seemingly at random and with no solid rationale, to found a spiritual movement that will include the very people he has been brought up to avoid. The command to this ordinary, unimaginative, and uncharismatic laborer to accompany Jesus might be worded today: "Follow me . . . and I will make you a fisherman of microcultures!"

Jesus' renaming of Simon as "Peter," and his statement that "on this 'rock' I will build my church" (Matt. 16:18), are usually taken to be solemn declarations that Peter will lay the solid foundation that will resist future persecution and create a global institution. I think Jesus was joking. It is both an illustration of God's sense of humor and a declaration that grace alone will guide the future Christian movement, that Jesus ironically and teasingly nicknames the future movement leader after an inert, immovable, lump of cooled lava. After all, Peter quickly lives up to his nickname.

When Jesus is transfigured on the mountaintop, Peter misses the significance entirely and immediately wants to buy property, obtain a mortgage, and build a pavilion in which God could reside. Presumably, it would have pews, stained glass, and a priesthood to keep the candles lit. It is much the same inclination of traditional, denominational church developers. Their first instinct is to find suitable property near a busy intersection, subsidize the salary and benefits of a seminary graduate, and gather folks inside the pavilion.

Peter never really "gets it" until quite some time after the Resurrection. Even after Jesus commands the disciples to carry the gospel on the road to all nations, Peter *still* retreats to the upper room to do strategic planning. In much the same way today, leaders of organized religion *still* beckon the judicatories to the central office to review the demographics and build consensus around tactics designed to reach out to the world without alarming those who already have membership privileges.

Even after the Holy Spirit is poured out, and people speak in the tongues of many nations, Peter still doesn't "get it." He gathers everybody inside the Jerusalem church and organizes great potluck suppers and begins "blending" worship so that both Hellenists and Jews, and the various generations in their families, have something to like in a one-size-fits-all church experience. When the inevitable politics arise, and factions begin jockeying for power to control the programs dedicated to their needs, Peter does what denominations do: he creates another layer of management. Certainly he is generous about it. The deacons mostly represent the minority Hellenists.

One senses a certain frustration in Scripture, as if God's sense of humor is wearing thin. Here is Peter wasting his time in Solomon's Portico debating with theologians and hobnobbing with Gamaliel. There is Peter sidetracked into the institution and angry that Ananias and Sapphira haven't lived up to their end of the stewardship campaign. There goes Peter on a weekend excursion to the Samaritans—who through no great effort of Peter's have managed to hear the gospel—in order to ensure their faith is politically correct and dogmatically pure. By the eighth chapter of Acts, God is getting frustrated. God sends an angel to the apostle Philip (the one apostle who had the gumption to go to the

Samaritans) with the peremptory command to "get up and go toward the south" to the wilderness road from Jerusalem to Gaza.

The tone of the command to "get up and go!" is that of a parent telling the kids to turn the television off and go outside to play. Unlike my children, Philip got up and went. The result is the conversion and baptism of the Ethiopian financier. It is interesting that God does not bother sending Philip back to Jerusalem this time, but "snatches him away" to the gentile towns of Azotus and Caesarea. God has more radical measures planned for Peter than another strategic planning meeting.

Peter's life is finally changed with a vision on a rooftop in Joppa in which he sees a large tablecloth coming down from heaven on which are collected all the creatures of the cultural forest. To Peter these are unclean, but God says "What God has made clean, you must not call profane" (Acts 10:15). God removes the artificial boundaries between sacred space, time, and people and secular space, time, and people and declares all cultural forms to be suitable vehicles for the Holy. This vision happens three times just to make sure Peter gets the point. Then the agents of centurion Cornelius arrive. They take a somewhat bewildered Peter back to Caesarea to the home of his national enemy, where he is received with considerable hospitality and great expectation. The Holy Spirit is poured out even before any water is splashed, and Peter *finally* gets it. God shows no partiality. Any person can be acceptable. Any lifestyle can connect with Christ. Any cultural form can be used to communicate God's redemptive power.

Now that Peter understands what it really means "to go unto all nations," baptizing strangers and accompanying Jesus on the road to mission, the subsequent persecution of the disciples and their expulsion from Jerusalem isn't so bad. James is killed, Peter is imprisoned and miraculously freed, and then relocates to Caesarea among the gentiles. Yet his attitude change makes all the difference. He does not see himself as a "church in exile," but rather as a church "on the road." Later, when Paul and Barnabas are recalled to the head office, it is Peter who comes to their rescue. The head office is upset that Paul and Barnabas are not teaching gentiles to be good Jews (circumcising them, teaching them the dietary laws, organizing them with a denominational polity, and coaching them to appreciate organ music). Peter helps James and the others to accept and affirm the mission to the gentiles, and the gospel truly takes flight to all the microcultures on earth. It took awhile, but the church finally got it right.

Legend has it that Peter went on to be a "rolling stone," that in the future he steadfastly refused "to gather moss." Peter turns up on the Appian Way outside of Rome, sees Jesus passing in the express lanes, and shouts *Quo Vadis, Domine?* Jesus responds that he is going into Rome (not away from Rome, and certainly not back to the denominational headquarters in Jerusalem), and Peter turns around to accompany him. There Peter is martyred. The legend states that Peter requested to be crucified upside down because he was not worthy to be killed in the same manner as his Lord. I suspect that he made this request as a way of celebrating how his life had been turned upside down.

## The Fragile Hope

The first sixteen chapters of the Acts of the Apostles are being reenacted today. Jesus again commands the disciples to "go unto all nations and microcultures." The denominations again retreat to the upper room to do demographic research and strategic planning. They interpret the command to mean that they must persuade, convince, cajole, trick, or manipulate the general public to come into the church, where they can be decently organized by a polity, coached to appreciate classical hymnology, enlisted to implement an institutional agenda, and enrolled in the stewardship campaign. Once the people are drawn in, churches "blend" the one and only option for worship, trying to appeal to every generation and every personal need all at once. They endure conflict amid controllers who are all competing to have the lion's share of the budget for their tastes and needs. And they add multiple layers of management, usually with benevolent affirmative action in favor of the Hellenists and other "people of color" (i.e., people who are not "our color").

It doesn't work, it misses the point, and God is getting frustrated. Just like in the old days, denominations plant a few churches out there among the Samaritans. Those church plants grow, reports about the Holy Spirit abound, the judicatory sends out the early Peter to ensure that they are all politically correct and dogmatically pure, all the institutional paraphernalia crushes the spirit, and the newly planted churches languish or die. The Spirit motivates congregational mavericks to "get up and go" to whatever "wilderness road" is convenient, and there these maverick churches acquaint strangers with Christ and baptize them any way they can. Yet the denomination isolates them, blocks them, criticizes them, excludes them, and manipulates capital funding and personnel policies to bring them back to Jerusalem.

Meanwhile, today's Peter is on the rooftop praying. The tablecloth with all the critters of the cultural forest is coming down. Indeed, the diverse microcultures are flowing through the urban gates, multiplying like rabbits on the land, and mass-migrating to the smallest towns. God keeps shouting that whatever *God* chooses can be a vehicle for the Holy. God has shouted this once. God has shouted this twice. God is shouting this thrice. And meanwhile, political forces again become more adversarial to Christianity and any form of organized religion. Persecution mounts as municipal planners withdraw property from availability to the church, boards of education refuse schools to be used for worship, door-to-door visitation is banned as an invasion of privacy, nontaxable benefits for clergy and churches are limited or slowly withdrawn, and the general public has moved from neutrality to hostility toward organized religion. The church is about to be thrown out of the office and onto the street, and God's unanswered question is *Will they lament their exile or hit the road into mission?*

There is hope, but it is fragile. More and more leaders are willing to be mavericks. More and more churches are ready to be road runners. More and more "Peters" are finally seeing the tablecloth, and hearing the voice. They are opening the door, and accompanying complete strangers to visit their worst enemies. They are mingling with people they used to dislike or even resent, but finding themselves welcomed to address a spiritual yearning that is profoundly deep. They are experiencing the power of God seizing upon their most timid actions and most modest words, and opening the floodgates of grace to the institutional "outsiders" to religion. Such experiences are absolutely astonishing to the already circumcised. Individual Christian leaders are experiencing their own *"Quo Vadis Moment,"* and saying with holy awe "Can anyone withhold the water for baptizing these people who have received the Holy Spirit just as we have?" (Acts 10:47).

My own life has experienced more than one such *Quo Vadis Moment.* God can choose the most unlikely settings to reveal the tablecloth descending from heaven. Long ago I spent summers leading ecumenical evangelism teams in the region above Detroit known as the "Top O' the Thumb." This is a region of small towns, cottages, and campgrounds about an hour and a half above Detroit on Saginaw Bay. Leaders taught children, intervened in personal crises, and led worship in the campgrounds.

It was my custom to visit one particular campground each Saturday evening. I would stroll among the campsites, introduce myself, and invite the folks to worship in the central pavilion the next morning. One Saturday I stayed longer than usual, and subsequently felt more tired than usual Sunday morning. As I walked through the campground in the morning it took me awhile to realize the campground clientele had changed overnight. After I had left the previous night, a Detroit bike gang had moved into the campground, and all the people I had visited had left. The gang had apparently been partying, drinking, doping, and carousing all night. It was now about eight o'clock on Sunday morning, and I was ambling through the park, tinkling a little bell, summoning God's people to sing "Kum Ba Yah" in the central pavilion.

Just at the moment when I realized my peril, and was about to turn back for Jerusalem, one of the bikers emerged from his pup tent by his motorcycle. He was the largest human being I had ever seen. It took him awhile to focus on me. He wasn't angry or annoyed, just mystified. He stared at me awhile, let out an enormous belch, and said the words that changed my life (again): "What the hell are you doing here?"

This is a *Quo Vadis Moment.* Peter was probably no less terrified when the agents of the centurion Cornelius summoned him from the rooftop in Joppa. As it turned out, the biker spent about two hours talking with me in the pavilion, telling me about his life, his addiction, and what it was like to love his woman and raise his little boy in the midst of social rejection, chronic crime, and constant violence. It left me at a turning point in my life. The campground had become a kind of microcosm of mission. I had to ask myself: Do I want to invest my energies ringing bells to summon all nations to sing one kind of music inside a central pavilion? Or do I want to run with Jesus, among any and all microcultures, helping them experience Christ on their own turf?

Many church leaders experienced that kind of *Quo Vadis Moment* in the weeks after the terrorist attacks of September 11, 2001. Thousands of lapsed Christians and basic pagans flocked into church with questions they couldn't answer, brokenness that they couldn't heal, and emptiness that they couldn't fill only to be met by very friendly greeters with pews they needed to fill, committees for which they needed volunteers, and organ music they wanted people to appreciate. So most of those newcomers left the central pavilion never to return, leaving many of the clergy and key lay leaders of the congregation asking the question: "What in heaven's name are we doing here?"

## *The Uncertain Momentum*

If the hope of future Christian mission in North America lies in more and more leaders experiencing the *Quo Vadis Moment,* the fragility of that hope is revealed by the uncertainty over whether or not traditional congregations and denominations will support, affirm, and follow those leaders. In other words, will the "moment" generate a "momentum"?

Recently The Weather Channel aired a film clip about mountain climbing. Cameras followed veteran climbers during a particularly difficult ascent up a sheet of ice. Do not stop. Do not look down. Keep going. After the initial foothold on the cliff face, the climbers gradually gained momentum in their ascent to the top. But during the climb, the weather changed dramatically. Temperatures eventually hovered just at freezing, clouds formed, and a steady drizzle descended on the climbers. Within twenty feet of the top, the veterans called a halt and descended safely to the cliff base. Why?

The ropes had become so encrusted with ice as to be nearly inflexible. The very clothes of the climbers, designed for the worst weather, had become like the chain mail armor of medieval times. Unable to lift an arm without the greatest effort, and fearing that the once flexible ropes would literally shatter, these veterans wisely descended to wait for a better day. It would come. A few days or a few weeks would pass, and they would successfully complete their historic ascent.

The situation is somewhat different for the church at the beginning of the new millennium. It is worse. Local churches continue to ascend the cliff face of mission in North America. Inch by inch, foothold by foothold, they each find their own contextual way to leverage themselves upward toward a fuller, deeper, bigger experience of being God's community. A budget placed here. A curriculum change placed there. A new hymnbook, an additional staff person, an alternate worship service, a paved parking lot, a streamlined board—all are placed according to an incremental plan to reach the summit of each congregation's potential. Leaders gaze up from their strategic plans, trying to anticipate the next challenge.

Just as they are making progress, the cultural climate changes. Some positions on the cliff face are more sheltered than others, so that some climbers feel the changed climate conditions more quickly or slowly than others. Their reaction to the changing conditions differs according to the climber's personality. Some churches sense the weather change and climb faster, becoming more and more exhausted, convinced that if they can just attain one more plateau everything will be fine. Other churches pin themselves to the relative shelter of a minor cultural crevice, set as many pitons as possible, build a little shelter to protect the climbing party from the cold, and wait. As the cultural climate becomes increasingly hostile to Christian mission, churches find the ascent increasingly difficult.

Churches began the ascent up the new millennium of mission in earnest after the Second World War. Everyone was filled with confidence. Some churches were already one hundred years old or more, and believed that the climbing tactics that had worked on other mountains would serve them well again. Other churches were expansion churches born of the financial reserves of a growing denomination, or the enthusiasm of a charismatic leader, and they were confident that the subsidies would always help them and the leader would always take care of them. All seemed well. The ascent proceeded according to plan. Then the weather changed.

Mainstream denominations numerically peaked in the late 1960s. Although many evangelical denominations continued to grow numerically well into the 1980s and 1990s, discipleship declined. The lifestyle commitment, spiritual depth, family values, passion for mission, love for the church universal, and readiness to volunteer were increasingly in short supply. It became harder and harder to recruit Sunday school teachers, board members, and committee chairpersons, even though people apparently had more free time. It became harder and harder to meet the operating budget and achieve the capital funding target, even though people apparently had more money to spend. Climbers ascending the millennial mountain had fewer pitons and less rope, increasing fatigue and dizziness, and more uncertainty about precisely where to place the next anchor to lever the church forward one more notch.

In the early days of the ascent, membership growth and program development helped the church ascend the mountain. "Church" was so popular that one's membership in it was expected. Anybody and everybody joined the church. The only real questions were about the best strategic plan to climb the cliff face, what kind of programmatic equipment to use in doing it, and how to obtain the best information-giving preacher to teach you how to do it. Then the weather changed.

- Pastors habitually inflated worship attendance statistics, taking the best Sundays in November as the norm, and ignoring the poor worship attendance the rest of the year.
- Boards constantly misjudged membership statistics, assuming an exclusive allegiance to their church, when in fact, members were committed to a variety of groups, ministries, or experiences that were often more meaningful.
- Sunday schools relied on youth to teach classes for which no adults volunteered, and the ill-equipped youth were motivated to do it because they were bored to tears by the worship service and longing to get out.
- Nurseries expected young parents to take turns caring for the kids, despite the fact that young parents had been doing exactly that all week and were yearning for some "adult reflection time." The same worship members who claimed to love kids refused to become involved in their care during worship, and instead became annoyed when they cried.

In the first years of the new millennium, formerly confident climbers are just trying to fill the committee vacancies, rescue a handful of core programs, and survive.

In the early days of the ascent, denominational helpers stood below and above ready to feed more rope, guide the placement of the next piton, or just send up sandwiches. Then the weather changed.

- Capital expansion subsidies from the judicatories diminished, capital costs multiplied exponentially, and competition for sparse resources dramatically increased.

- Judicatory vision from above and below became so obscured by the weather that by doggedly following strategic plans without contextual verification, it became the least reliable guide to placing the next piton, much to the sorrow and frustration of the climbers.
- Different conditions on the cliff face called for new technologies and tactics, but judicatories kept sending up the same old pitons and shouting down the same old instructions.
- Diminished income and burdensome bureaucracy not only reduced staffing, but redeployed the remaining staff away from the cliff face, resulting in fewer people below and above supporting the struggling climbers.

In the first years of the new millennium, formerly confident climbers are realizing that the supply lines are unreliable and they are on their own.

In the early days of the ascent, there were many climbers. Seminaries graduated large numbers of fresh-faced, first-career, eager clergy, swelling the ranks of local ministerial associations. At the same time, churches seemed to spring up on every corner, in every subdivision, in glorious redundancy. Then the weather changed.

- Seminaries taught ecclesiology as a means to missiology, equipping churches to only climb Mount Everest the way Edmund Hillary and his Sherpa guides did long ago.
- Fewer leaders sought ordination, and the few who did were often more interested in the art of clinging to a rock face than reaching the top, more fascinated by wearing mountain climbing apparel than placing a piton, more eager to send up sandwiches from below and shout orders from the top than hold a rope, or more passionate about deriding the people sending sandwiches from below and shouting orders from the top than setting an anchor.

- Judicatory affiliations and local church networks dissolved into competition for resources, and fragmented into ideologically driven disputes, so that whatever the danger of falling might be, "at least, by God, we won't resort to using the color of rope *those* people use!"

In the first years of the new millennium, some climbers have fallen to their death, some cling to the cliff face in resigned righteousness, some wait vainly for the denomination to rescue them, some pool their resources with other climbers to last a little longer, some pirate the resources of fallen comrades to occupy a sheltered position, some climb down and declare congregational life a waste of time, and yes, a few find a way to keep climbing to the top. Once there were many climbers, and now there are fewer.

The situation of the church at the turn of the millennium is worse than the plight of the rock climbers on the Discovery Channel. The rock climbers will wait a few days or a few weeks, the weather will clear, and they will try again.

Then again, what if this weather change is not just the result of an alternation in the prevailing wind, which will switch back again in a few days? What if the weather change is the first dramatic sign of a new ice age that will last for fifteen thousand years? What if the climbers discover that they themselves have precipitated a permanent climatic change due to their own habits of climbing or abuse of the cliff face? What if the new ice age is partly the result of a global warming for which human society is largely to blame?

The irony is that the very strengths that made the church great in the nineteenth and early twentieth centuries are making the church weak at the beginning of the twenty-first century. Not only has the cultural climate changed, but also the very institutional success of the church has helped that change come about.

- The redundant management style that worked so successfully to grow denominations has left behind a trail of burned-out, disillusioned people alienated from the institution they once loved.

- The classic, presentational worship experience that once brought the family together now just exacerbates the growing gaps between subcultures.
- The laborious certification process that once guaranteed quality in pastoral leadership now simply guarantees that by the time the clergy are certified they are already out of date.
- The generic denominational mission funding strategy that once pooled enormous capital to leverage positive change around the globe cannot amass sufficient wealth or motivate sufficient energy to intervene in a neighborhood crisis.

What worked for the church in previous centuries now works against the church. The trail of frustrated, disappointed, or indifferent people left behind by the church has helped create this changed climate. Never before has the public been so interested in spiritual things, and never before has it been so alienated from the institutional church. There is enormous interest in climbing the mountain, but no confidence that the church has chosen the right cliff face, created the right strategy, produced the best equipment, or trained the best leaders.

Now here is the irony. My experience as a consultant with churches large and small, of all brand names across North America, has taught me that almost everyone will agree that the above analysis of the general contemporary situation is true, but few churches are convinced that it applies to them in particular. Most people readily agree that "the church" should change, and few people are willing to risk changing *their* church. Individual leaders (clergy or laity or both) experience the *Quo Vadis Moment,* but the combination of cultural hostility to Christian mission, denominational obsession with top-down control, and the self-interest of veteran congregational members blocks leaders from ever building *Quo Vadis Momentum.* They may make progress ascending the cliff face of postmodern mission for a time, but leadership eventually exhausts itself negotiating the cultural hurdles, quarreling with judicatories over resources, and hauling up the deadweight of listless laity and career clergy who may want to celebrate at the top but don't want to share in the climb.

There are exceptions, of course, and these churches are becoming the "teaching churches" in the postdenominational and post-seminary spiritual world that is emerging. I have written about these churches elsewhere. (See *Kicking Habits: Upgrade Edition* [Nashville: Abingdon Press, 2001] and *Growing Spiritual Redwoods* [with William Easum] [Nashville: Abingdon Press, 1997].) Most of these churches have succeeded in change, however, by paying a price in stress, division, and marginalization from their parent denominations.

Many churches, of course, never even attempt to climb. They prefer to camp at the foot of the mountain, preferably where they can get the best view, and memorialize "St. Edmund of Hillary and his spiritual Sherpas" with brass plaques and high liturgies. Occasionally they pay professionals to attempt a climb (missionaries, youth pastors, outreach agencies, and the like), but rarely do they provide sufficient resources and the climbers either fall to their doom or cut the rope to the parent church and network with faith-based nonprofits. The churches themselves are simply in a state of denial. It may be due to corporate addiction, corporate senility, the pursuit of political agendas, or sheer spiritual laziness. If they are historic churches, remote churches, or politically significant churches, denominations tend to feed that denial by providing financial subsidies to shore up an institutional disaster. "Everything is fine here!" the leaders say. The congregation is aging, fewer people worship, less money is invested in mission, innumerable committees exist in name only, the organization runs a chronic operating deficit, and nobody on the street can remember where the church is located if they are asked, but "everything is fine here!"

Most churches are in a third category. These are small, medium, and even large congregations that consider themselves "traditional" in whatever definition they wish to use that word. The self-description "traditional" really means that they are "progressive conservatives who welcome the public to share the privileges of membership." They enjoy a degree of stability and reasonable corporate health.

- Worship participation is often at least 35 percent of capacity, and on high holy days these churches need extra chairs.
- They field a reasonable choir for Sunday morning that sings traditional music well.
- They have a youth group—a small one with unpopular kids or a large one with popular kids.
- They have achieved an organizational equilibrium in which a small board endures only a few serious vacancies that can still be filled in a pinch by veterans.
- They keep the building in good repair, pay salaries, give up to 3 percent of their budget to mission, readily respond to local crises, and operate an aggressive retail campaign to compensate for any operating deficit in the fall.
- The pastor has a reasonably happy relationship with the congregation and has at least five years of tenure, marred by nothing worse than chronic complaints from a handful of needy people that "the minister doesn't visit enough."
- The congregation enjoys relative harmony, people get along with one another, and the potluck suppers, afterservice coffee hours, and other fellowship experiences are warm and inviting.

Longtime members of these churches will be aware that the church is not what it was in the late 1960s. They may lament the smaller Sunday school, the diminished youth participation, the lesser quality organ music, the reduced staff. And they may complain that sports has usurped sacred time on Sunday morning, and that the pastor spends too much time on judicatory business. Nevertheless, life in these churches is still pretty good. They have good fellowship, solid biblical preaching, and are satisfied that they have indeed done something to benefit society local and global.

These are the churches that say to the consultant: "Why should we change?" Perhaps the prevailing cultural winds will return to normal, and everybody will come back to church again. Even if the prevailing winds last longer than expected, perhaps our role is to lean into it, remain stalwart, and resist being blown about by the trivialities of our context. Even if the prevailing wind turns into a tornado, perhaps it is better to die faithful in Kansas than risk being transported to Oz.

Yet the stress of change is building even in these churches. As the years (and now months, and even weeks) roll by, the categories of congregational life are changing. It used to be that the congregation could be divided by age (adults, youth, children), by length of membership (veterans and newcomers), by office (elders, deacons, and members), or by participation (resident active members, resident inactive members, nonresident members, adherents). Now all those boundaries are blurring or disappearing. Today there are three categories of people in these seemingly healthy churches:

1. *The Restless Ones:* About 20 percent of the congregation (young or old, veteran or newcomer, officer or member, active or inactive) are so restless that if "things do not change" in the next few months, they will step backward from their connection to the church. These people may not know exactly what needs to be changed or how, but they are convinced that there is a higher calling, a bigger mission, and a better way to be the church.

2. *The Controllers:* Another 20 percent or more of the congregation (in the same blurred diversity as before) consider the church the one unchanging rock in the turmoil of their lives. They want to bend the congregation's life and mission to match their personal agendas. That might mean that the church must remain the same, or that the church must return to the personally selected heritage (chosen from a number of optional heritages) that suits the controllers' particular mythol-

ogy, or that the church must adopt a particular programmatic agenda that is in the best interest of the controller and his or her family.

Note: The Controllers are in constant and increasingly stressful negotiation with the Restless Ones. Sometimes they are perceived as dictatorial blockers to change, but other times they form alliances around particular programmatic adjustments in which the self-interest of the Controllers and the higher calling of the Restless Ones seem for once to be on converging paths. That is why a Restless One surprisingly finds himself or herself "on the board" instead of on the fringe where he or she might have expected to be. The Restless One today can be subverted to become the Controller of tomorrow, just as the Controller today may pose as the Restless One of tomorrow.

3. *The In-Betweens:* About 60 percent of the congregation are in a continuum between restlessness and control. Unlike the Controllers, these are healthy people, in the sense that they are reasonably open to unfamiliar and uncomfortable ideas. They may be cautious, unimaginative, and not particularly knowledgeable, but they are teachable, coachable, trainable people. Unlike the Restless Ones, these are contented people, in the sense that they are basically satisfied with worship, leadership, and membership expectations. They may be opinionated about music, nervous that the pastor wears blue jeans, and critical of the old sound system, but they will accept aesthetically displeasing experiences for the sake of the youth, overlook the pastoral dress code for the sake of great preaching and quality crisis intervention, and commit to incremental five-year strategic plans.

Note: The In-Betweens are in increasingly stressful interaction with the other two groups. Controllers bargain with them to be elected to office, provided they guarantee a reasonable facsimile of the status quo.

Restless Ones woo them to espouse a new cause, disguising the fact that the "new cause" may eventually revolutionize the church with which they are so content. In-Betweens regard Controllers at best as "sound ecclesiastical leaders" and at worst as "inflexible idiots." They regard Restless Ones at best as "prophets" and at worst as just plain "nuts."

The congregation today is divided among these three groups. The old statistics of age, membership, group participation, office, or marital status are all irrelevant compared to this. Someone is going to leave the church in the next few months or years. If things don't change, the Restless Ones will leave, and they will take some of the In-Betweens with them. If things do change, the Controllers will leave, and they will take some of the In-Betweens with them. There really is no alternative.

This book is aimed at that 60 percent of the reasonably stable, healthy congregation who are the "In-Betweens" of the changing millennium, and at the church leaders who are trying to convince, coach, and guide them to prosper in every sense of that word. It is not aimed at churches that are in absolute denial, and their leaders will no doubt demand proof for every assertion made, and steadfastly ignore it when it is provided. Nor is this book aimed at churches that have radically transformed to thrive in whatever way is contextual for them in the new age; their leaders will likely find this discussion dull. I write for the majority of healthy Christians, in the majority of reasonably stable churches that are all clinging to a rope part way up the cliff face of the postmodern world.

The fragile hope of mission in North America is that somehow this 60 percent can share a *Quo Vadis Moment*, and build *Quo Vadis Momentum*.

# Two

# THE FRAGILE ORGANIZATION

Chroniclers of ancient times speak with mingled terror and awe of a weapon of war called "Greek Fire." The tiniest spark could start a fire on a ship or in a castle that would rapidly spread and consume anything in its path. The most alarming thing about Greek Fire, however, was that it could not be extinguished by water. In fact, water seemed to make the fire even fiercer. The more water, the bigger the flame! The recipe for Greek Fire was lost in the Dark Ages, but it has been rediscovered today in a different form. Today it is a fire that consumes not warships or castles, but church organizations.

It is a fire of discontent. The tiniest spark (a missed pastoral visit, a quarrel over hymnbooks, an untoward comment) can start a fire that spreads quickly and consumes all in its path. It may spread to the operating budget (causing a deficit), from thence to the Sunday school (causing a curriculum crisis), then on to the worship service (causing a quarrel over the proper method of serving Holy Communion), erupt in the board (causing a power struggle), and ultimately singe the pastoral relationship (causing personnel to go on disability). Along the way, this Greek Fire of discontent has consumed the attention of the church veterans, alienated newcomers who quickly smell the smoke, and severed the last tie holding eager members longing for real spirituality from the institution that once provided it.

In response to this new form of Greek Fire, congregations and middle judicatories have multiplied management, tightened supervision, created elaborate governance processes, and deployed endless listening teams. "Accountability" is now the word spoken at congregational and denominational meetings more often than any other (including words like "forgiveness," "grace," and "acceptance"). The terrifying reality, however, is that the normal "water" of organizational procedure does *not* seem to put out the fire!

- Congregations rewrite job descriptions, but workloads are even larger and more confused.
- Churches streamline constitutions, but meetings multiply.
- Judicatories establish stricter personnel policies, but abuses and litigations increase.
- Nominations processes are expanded, but the number of volunteers decreases.
- Stewardship becomes more aggressive, but receipts remain stagnant or diminish.
- Technology and office space are updated, but efficiency goes down.

In fact, the more churches talk about "accountability," and the more ad hoc committees are multiplied, and the more intentional the church becomes about governance, the more intense the fire becomes.

## The Cult of Harmony

The explanation of this terrifying mystery lies in understanding the nature of the Christian church as the "official religion" of the contemporary pagan world. What started as a movement on the roads of the Roman Empire to share the welcome relief of Jesus

Christ has gone far beyond institutionalization. The Christian church has become just another cult in the pagan world. It is not the cult of Roma, or the cult of Cybele. It is the cult of harmony.

Traditional church institutions of the nineteenth and twentieth centuries lived in a culturally homogeneous, relatively slow-paced world, in which most problems could be solved by increased education, the investment of extra time, some cooperative common sense, and tender loving pastoral care. The Christian education committee, communications committee, and visitation committee were the most important groups in the church organization, and were also the prestige power positions. Finance committees methodically harvested money, professional office staff coordinated affairs, and the trustees made sure everything was legal. The denomination and the board supplied the mission. The pastor shepherded *his* (and later, *her*) flock, which generally stayed together, through all the life cycles until they died.

The "harmony" of the traditional church enjoyed by parents, grandparents, and great-grandparents is probably more real in the nostalgic imagining of baby boomers than it was to their ancestors. After all, the delegates to the First Continental Congress in 1774 hesitated to even offer a prayer to open the proceedings lest Presbyterians, Episcopalians, Catholics, Quakers, and various nonconformists be offended. In the chaotic, culturally diverse world of contemporary post-war builders and baby boomers, however, the seeming harmony of our ancestors seems a veritable Eden to which baby boomers long to return. The seeming agreement about daily behavior and the seeming concord about religious doctrine represent the real vision of many churches. Please note that I'm not speaking about any *particular* behavior or doctrine, but about the *agreement* and *concord* itself. It is the "feeling" or the "spirit" of harmony that is admired. It is the new god of official religion in pagan North America.

The contemporary bureaucracies and hierarchies that thought of themselves as "traditional" made a cult out of "harmony." The ideal was for a church "family" to all gather "intergenerationally," smile a lot and politely "pass the peace," speak when spoken to, manage by consensus, and chant "They'll know we are Christians by our love" (i.e., people will know we are Christians by our internal organizational affection among the resident members and regular worshipers).

Consider this typical story of Greek Fire in a traditional church organization.

St. Harmonious-by-the-Lake Church considers itself a "family" church. They do the same blended worship service twice (and only on Sundays), designed so that there is a little bit of music for young and old alike. They "pass the peace" with a smile, staff the church with a pastor (to preach and visit) and Christian education minister (to run the Sunday school and youth groups). They rent space to a day care center. As the millennium turns, the cult of harmony is shattered.

The pastor finds himself or herself doing more funerals, and constantly feels guilty that he or she cannot keep up with hospital and home visitation. More than this, complaints about pastoral care multiply in the board meetings and through the grapevine. *He doesn't visit me. She isn't helpful enough. He doesn't stay long enough. She doesn't pray enough.* The pastor begins to think (guiltily) that he is not *paid* enough! Worse yet, government agencies simultaneously download counseling and intervention responsibilities from beleaguered social services, *and* raise the standard of counseling and care so that the pastor is constantly worrying about litigation.

The worship attendance in both services plateaus and declines. The one-size-fits-all church doesn't fit anybody, but each person seems to want everybody else to wear his or her size! *The music is too traditional. The music is too contemporary. The service is too long. The sermons are too boring, too political, too irrelevant. The children aren't cute* and *quiet.* Boards endlessly debate whether to serve Communion by tray or intinction. Church veterans grumble that worship "doesn't feel reverent anymore" and newcomers are suddenly bold enough to ask the greeter "Why should I bother coming here?"

Adherents resist regulation. Not only is the members' median age rising, but more and more people unaccountably want to participate and make decisions without actually joining the church. Boards split hairs over resident and nonresident lists, and the definition of "active" or "inactive" membership. People want to vote, but won't attend. Officers want to shape policy, but won't worship. The program year when one can expect to make decisions, learn stuff, or do things is compressed to as little as four out of twelve months. Consensus management requires so many people that as long as you are willing to use offering envelopes and show up occasionally, you're in!

The budget conflates into one capital pool for church maintenance. Money can be raised easily for a new roof, but not for a new ministry. First, the boundaries between the property fund and the memorial fund are blurred. The church begins dedicating the new kitchen faucet in loving memory of someone's aunt. If the beloved niece objects (and she will), she is told that God's Temple as a whole is a heritage to be protected. Then the boundaries between property and personnel are blurred. Professionals are needed to care for the members, perpetuate bequests, and keep the doors open in a "ministry of presence." If mission units object (and they will), they are told that the church "family" is the fundamental mission unit of the church.

Greek Fire continues to spread through St. Harmonious-by-the-Lake. Veterans grumble, adherents grow resentful, newcomers chide, staff compete, factions struggle, and members drift. Yet the cult of harmony remains the mythological center of congregational life. If the middle judicatory responds to the crisis, the church family closes ranks and declares everything to be just fine. On Christmas Eve and Mothers Day worshipers gather to sing the old songs, weep, and embrace one another. The in-group of lay leaders loves one another deeply, and complains that it has to do all the work. The staff, guilt-ridden and frustrated, begins to consider early retirement or a career change.

Most church leaders are aware that music is the number one issue that divides churches today. They are also aware that this is because music has become a lightning rod for cross-generational feuding, and that as new "generations" with new attitudes, fashions, and perspectives emerge every three years, the fight over music only gets worse. However, church leaders are often unaware that music has become the lightning rod of controversy *because the contemporary church is obsessed with the cult of harmony.* Music is the ultimate "feel good" medium of harmony. Churches prize the combination of simultaneously sounded notes that produce chords and chord progressions that have a pleasing effect. They admire the gowned choirs, and appreciate the ordered rows of singers, all holding the same hymnal and singing the same tune. The six-year-old cherubs lined at the front struggling through "Jesus Loves Me" are a sign of hope to the congregation who care little about the words but enjoy the *harmony!*

Experience in hundreds of small and large churches leads me to speculate that this is why organ music in particular is so controversial. The organ is perhaps the instrument par excellence producing "harmony." When church people listen to an organ, no matter how elaborate with pipes or electronics, they actually imagine a "harmonium." Indeed, in many small churches on Christmas Eve and other significant occasions, the church will actually use the long-neglected instrument. The "harmonium" is a keyboard instrument in which the notes are produced by air driven through metal reeds by bellows operated by the feet, in short, an early organ. This unique blend of nostalgia and lyric epitomizes the cult of harmony. Our ancestors did occasionally sing "Silent Night" on Christmas Eve (although usually preferring other more aggressively theological hymns requiring a fifty-two-week background of spiritual discipline in order to understand). These hymns could be played with an out-of-tune violin or broken down saxophone. The contemporary cult of harmony, however, demands that "Silent Night" be the centerpiece of the Christmas service. It demands little theological training to understand, and motivates occasionally worshiping church members to hold hands, sway to the music, and weep.

## *The Paradox of Concord*

The paradox of the cult of harmony is that inevitably it becomes regulatory. The more slippery that "feeling of harmony" becomes, the more energetic church leaders become to generate it, maintain it, and actually enforce it. This explains the peculiarity of the contemporary church that is simultaneously so laissez-faire about attendance, behavior, and belief, and yet so passionate about uniformity in voting, public policy, and worship. *We are all one happy family here, and by God, we'll do whatever it takes to keep it that way!*

Preoccupation with the good feeling of harmony actually drives the church toward control. It may be hierarchical control, or bureaucratic control, control by the oldest member, or control by the elected office, but church life in the cult of harmony is about control. The floor plans of our ancestors that were once designed for inexpensive seating and good acoustics have been converted by the cult of harmony into methodologies of control. In fact, today there are cheaper and better ways to seat people than in rows of wooden pews, and there are better, electronically enhanced ways to hear and see than by placing presenters in elevated pulpits, but the cult of harmony resists them. Why? Because the present floor plan enables better control and imposes better uniformity.

It is important to understand the special kind of uniformity that is being imposed by the cult of harmony. It is not really agreement about ideas, nor is it conformity about daily behavior, nor is it passionate pursuit of a common vision. It is uniformity around *aesthetics.* Contemporary churches of the cult of harmony are actually very unclear about shared expectations in daily behavior, essential beliefs that give strength in times of trouble, and motivating visions that shape individual lifestyles. Control is exercised in matters of taste, appearance, and sensibility.

## *Taste*

What is important to the cult of harmony is that members of the church family share the same discernment in art, media, and fashion when involved in church business. The boundaries of that uniformity may vary from church to church. One church might expect men to wear coat and tie to worship, but allow women to wear slacks; another church might welcome everyone in T-shirts, but reject tattoos. One church might emphasize classical music, but allow occasional rhythm and blues; another church may emphasize easy listening jazz, but ban hard rock. What is important is that the people of the church generally share similar aesthetic tastes.

Note especially that these shared tastes need not dominate a church member's private life. This is a shared taste when people are involved in church business. They may commonly listen to country music driving in their cars, but in church they accept the necessity of listening to classical music. They may wear different clothes, eat and drink different foods, even value different color schemes in decorating, but in church affairs they all accept an alternative aesthetic norm.

Church members can have remarkably different personal beliefs and behavior patterns, but it is matters of *taste* that cause trouble. The oddest things can be requested in weddings and funerals, but it is the demand to give a higher percentage of the budget to the R&B band than to the chancel choir that will provoke the strongest reaction. Departing too far from the shared aesthetic taste of the congregation will provoke the question *Are we being faithful?*

## *Appearance*

What is important to the cult of harmony is that members unite around public policy, not personal or daily behavioral expectations. In other words, church members must present the public appearance of unity around major issues, but are relatively free to live as they wish. Right-wing churches expect the congregation to be united around the sanctity of family life, but in daily experience unmarried cohabitation, separation and divorce, unrestricted discipline of children, relative indifference to the elderly, and limited sensitivity to teens are as prominent as in the rest of society. Left-wing churches expect the congregation to petition governments for the rights of the poor, but in daily experience members drive expensive cars, move to bigger houses, and take expensive vacations as does the rest of society.

The cult of harmony is not shallow, and the examples above are not intended to uncover some obvious hypocrisy. There will always be an ambiguity between ideal and reality, and people may well share an ideal to value life and still debate whether that implies a vegetarian diet. The point is that the cult of harmony does not see a need to reflect on that. Participants are concerned with their place in the world of public policy. They are concerned that outsiders perceive them to be uniformly of the same opinion on specific issues. What specific church members decide to do about an unexpected pregnancy may vary widely due to circumstance, but lobbying for the wrong political position will provoke the question *Are we being faithful?*

## Sensibility

What is important to the cult of harmony is not results, so much as the exercise of "common sense." This is really an aesthetic issue, not a parliamentary issue. The cult values sensible persons who can cooperate together to achieve sensible compromises. One must be open to emotional impressions, prioritize the feelings of others, and make decisions with the minimum of offense to other members of the church. General administrative and planning meetings are the proving grounds for such uniformity. The art of parliamentary procedure is not really to make the right decisions, but rather to make the best decision possible that alienates the fewest people.

Camaraderie, not strategy, is the essence of the cult of harmony. Moderation, balance, and continuity are crucial. These are aesthetic concerns, not moral concerns, because such priorities keep stress low and are less likely to disturb the harmony of the congregation. Men and women in the business world may take investment risks and make radical changes in the corporate world during the week, but become remarkably timid in the financial and strategic planning of the church on Sunday. The same audacity and aggressiveness that empowered product development and boosted income during the week, invites the question in the cult of harmony *Are we being faithful?*

The ability to distinguish between aesthetics and theology is not as easy as many church leaders might think. Aesthetic uniformity is no less passionate a quest than theological insight. Look at behavior. If uniformity of ideas were important, then everybody would be involved in adult continuing education. If uniformity in daily behavior were important, then mentoring and modeling by leadership would be crucial. If uniformity of vision were important, then clear and urgent corporate goals would literally reshape individual career paths and personal financial planning. None of this happens in the cult of harmony. Few adults are involved in serious spiritual growth disciplines. Leaders rarely mentor or model specifically Christian lifestyles. Church mission statements do not alter many career paths. Instead, the real centers of passion and interest for church members are oriented around worship (taste); property, marketing, advocacy, and preaching (appearance); and committee, board, or general meetings (sensibility).

The paradox of concord is that churches attempt to regulate a feeling, legislate a harmony, and enforce a spirit. In common pursuit of harmony, churches fracture through competing uniformities. This is the chemical formula for Greek Fire, the unstable combination of sentimentality and control. Congregations and judicatories do not try to address discontent in the church through adult spiritual growth, leadership creativity, and lay empowerment, but by imposing abstract standards of "good" liturgy and music, by coercing members to support particular public policies, and by multiplying meetings. Yet the discontent simply accelerates, because the chemical formula of the "water" is really just the same as the chemical formula of the "fire." The cult of harmony is already preoccupied with aesthetics of taste, appearance, and sensibility, and in response the church pours on additional aesthetics of taste, appearance, and sensibility. Poof!

## The Contradiction in Inclusivity

Modern churches (liberal or conservative) pride themselves in their openness and inclusivity. Every congregation claims to be welcoming and friendly to the full demographic diversity of the public. Few really are. The paradox of concord forces the cult of harmony to proclaim inclusive policies, and behave in exclusive ways. The liberal church claims to be open to people of all sexual orientations, but in fact includes few alternative lifestyles. The conservative church claims to be open to people of all cultures, races, and economic backgrounds, but in fact includes few socio-economic groups. The problem is not really latent homophobia or racism, but simply is the cult of harmony itself. Anyone, of any race and lifestyle, truly can join the church, *provided* he or she shares the same obsession with harmony and accepts the imposed aesthetic uniformity of taste, appearance, and sensibility. This may well exclude most people of alternate subcultures, but the underlying issue is not race or language. There will be a few people in the cult of harmony from other microcultures, but they will be the minority of their microculture who are comfortable with the cult of harmony of that particular church.

This contradiction in inclusivity is most obviously revealed in the resistance of modern churches to developing truly credible grievance procedures. The cult of harmony does little more than provide a suggestion box in the narthex or institute an ad hoc committee for investigating complaints or issue invitations from the pastor to "call any time with a concern." They never provide an accessible, trustworthy, thorough, and fair grievance procedure. So repressed are complaints, that when they finally do emerge they always erupt as major litigations that force the church from chronic denial. Churches lose members in these litigations, not because the lawsuit is justified or unjustified, but because the myth of harmony has been shattered.

Modern church bureaucracies and hierarchies may be benevolent, but deep inside they believe that if the church were really the church then a serious grievance procedure wouldn't be necessary. Discontent is simply not supposed to be part of church life. In the cult of harmony, three hidden assumptions dominate church life.

## 1. If you are discontented, don't complain. Leave.

All those redundant levels of management are designed to create the largest homogeneity possible. Look around in worship or congregational meetings and you may notice that people are generally of the same age, race, economic background, educational training, aesthetic preference, fashion consciousness, and ideological preference. If you are discontented in that group, *you just don't fit in.* That doesn't make you a bad person, but you are just not "our kind of people." Best that you move to another church. So long as culture kept feeding the church large quantities of new members, and denominations kept opening new congregational franchises, discontent could be avoided.

## 2. If you are discontented, don't complain. Join a committee.

The habit of organizational development is that the bigger the church becomes, the bigger the board must become. More people, more committees. The path to belonging to the "family" is to service the infrastructure of "family life." Traditional organizations assume that discontent is a result of misunderstanding. People must not be well informed. If only they joined a committee, they would understand the realities of church life and accept the decisions of the board or denomination. So long as culture believed that education was the ultimate cure for evil, and that the mere multiplication and communication of information could correct behavior, discontent could be avoided.

## 3. If you are discontented, don't complain. Make friends with the right people.

The centralization of traditional organizations means that power is passed on judiciously to the right people. Patriarchs birth more patriarchs, and matriarchs nurture more matriarchs. In order to get things done, one needs to know the right people, follow proper procedure, make the right phone call. The coffee-hour before the meeting is really more important than the meeting itself. Power is passed on by patronage. So long as cultural leaders were credibly caring, and culture itself seemed progressive, so that every day, in every way, every person could anticipate improving their lives even a little bit, discontent could be avoided.

In the cult of harmony, all the talk of "accountability" is at root grudging and reactionary. The church is *really* supposed to be one happy family. The hidden resentment of the church board is that if only "some people" would just "get with the program," we wouldn't have to do all this! The complaint box is buried in the narthex, and the complex denominational complaint procedures are never fully advertised or explained. The discontented should find a more congenial home, join the management, or attend a supper club.

The primary grievance process of the cult of harmony is the anonymous telephone campaign. It is anonymous, not because people are afraid to give their name, but because individuals really believe they are speaking for the whole church. The caller never says, "*I think* this should change," but rather "*People are saying* that this is wrong." It is a telephone campaign, rather than a personal confrontation or board resolution, because it seems less stressful and more sensible. It preserves the appearance of harmony, because both the anger expressed and the hurt received remain hidden.

The harmony of the modern church organization is very precarious today, however. The discontinuity between the real experience of culture and the mythology of church organizations has disastrous consequences. The more chaotic and diverse the world becomes, the more passionately modern church people cling to the cult of harmony. The obsession comes with a price that is increasingly too high to pay.

- Adult education shrinks in importance, and shifts emphasis from personal and spiritual growth to consciousness-raising and communicating a centrally controlled mission agenda.
- Worship is increasingly designed for assimilation rather than motivation, an acculturation process through which newcomers learn the tribal code and veterans celebrate membership privileges.
- Children and youth ministries are redirected to apprentice people under the age of eighteen to take organizational and financial responsibility for church programs, rather than grow Christian disciples fulfilling spiritual gifts and pursuing calls to ministry.
- Stewardship is limited to fund-raising for the budget, and has little to do with changing lifestyles.
- Pastoral visitation and one-to-one counseling overwhelm professional clergy's time and energy.
- Property maintenance oriented toward perpetuating sentimental attachments to the past becomes more important than property development that reshapes facilities and technologies for future mission.

The church pays the price for this obsession with harmony by leaving a trail of disenchanted adults, irrelevant worship, non-existent youth groups, chronic deficits, burned-out clergy, and historic mausoleums. At one time the prestige of the church in culture, the wealth of denominations, and the abundance of clergy could afford to pay that price, but no more.

## The Wasteful Organization

At first glance, the fragility of the organization has nothing to do with ecclesiology or theology. The organization is fragile because increasing numbers of people today refuse to participate in an organizational model that is worse than slow. It is abusive. It does not matter which denominational polity we are talking about, for they are all alike—bureaucracies and hierarchies that are intrinsically a waste of time and energy. The reason young and old decline to accept nominations, or refuse to pursue ordination, is that they simply do not want to squander their God-given gifts in fruitless meetings. The irrelevance and frustration of the ecclesiastical machine becomes even more clearly defined because young and old are experiencing quite different, more fulfilling organizational models in other walks of life.

The traditional church is like an inefficient gasoline engine that requires many gallons of fuel to operate, and discharges a cloud of noxious fumes. The gasoline engine was an acceptable means of transportation so long as the environment contained plenty of oil reserves and could accept limited pollution. Even so, the traditional church organization (with all of its boards, executives, trustees, standing committees, program committees, nominations committees, ad hoc committees, management levels, judicatories, offices, budget lines, and "turbo-charged" incremental plans) was an acceptable means of mission so long as Christendom provided plenty of new members and culture could accept limited numbers of burned-out lives. That time, however, is over.

The traditional church organization requires a huge input of volunteer labor. In fact, the smaller the church is (and over 80 percent of the churches in America have fewer than 350 participating adults), the larger the percentage of people required to service the church infrastructure. If you add up all the committees and offices and liaisons, over 50 percent of the congregation is required to fill vacancies for the organization to work at maximum efficiency. As the input diminishes, and the church "takes in" fewer members, fewer ordinands, and fewer volunteers, the faithful few are required to wear more hats, do more jobs, and attend more meetings, just to keep the machine running.

Traditional church organizations are becoming as obsessive about "getting people to come to church" as governments are about finding new reserves of crude oil. Those friendly greeters at the door have but one question in the back of their minds: What time and talents do these newcomers possess that can service our organizational needs, and how can we persuade these nice people to let us use them?

This, of course, is one reason why the megachurch has been so successful in recent decades. People feel that they are less likely to be lumbered with administrative responsibility, and will have more time to enjoy life. This is not a shallow aspiration. People really do yearn for joy, not drudgery, and they really do want to enjoy life in all of its holistic dimensions, not just go shopping.

Yet even the megachurch is proving to be less of a joy than participants expected. Those large buildings, professional staffs, satellite communications, state-of-the-art technologies, and comfortable chairs are increasingly expensive. Indeed, federal and regional governments are fast finding ways to tax, surcharge, and otherwise siphon money away from formerly protected religious groups, so that the cost of ministry is almost certainly going up and up in a world more hostile to organized religion. Those friendly greeters are now approaching people in the coffee shop and corporate boardrooms with but one question in the back of their minds: What financial resources do these newcomers possess that can fund our organizational needs, and how can we persuade these nice people to let us invest them?

The point is that the public is not stupid. It can sniff out a marketer a mile away. It does not take long for people to figure out what question lies in the back of a friendly greeter's mind. They know when they are being siphoned into a huge, hungry machine intent on institutional survival. They might actually be willing to accept this (since the huge growth in charitable giving suggests that the public is actually remarkably generous) if they are convinced that the ecclesiastical machine is going to produce something of importance. That confidence, however, has eroded dramatically.

If the public is alarmed by the enormous input of the ecclesiastical machine, it is also skeptical about its output. In a world of no-load investments, people are dismayed to see their leaders diverted into pointless denominational oversight and members' money deployed to support redundant levels of management. In a world of homelessness and hunger down the street, they are dismayed to see their money preserving useless heritage properties and nostalgic campgrounds. They suddenly realize they can get more bang for the charitable buck by giving money to an aggressive, faith-based, nonprofit parachurch than they can by giving to the generic denominational mission fund.

Even the megachurches are not immune to the growing skepticism regarding the output of ecclesiastical organizations. Amid small towns and urban neighborhoods increasingly stressed by racial and cross-cultural change, the public is wondering why megachurches can't seem to model healthy heterogeneity and mirror the ethnic, economic, and aesthetic diversity of the region or city. In the face of imminent environmental disaster, endemic poverty, and increasing violence, the public is wondering why megachurches can't seem to accomplish more than sending mission teams that build schools for a single village or clean the sand on a single beach, or that establish satellite uplinks to raise global awareness about Jesus. They suddenly realize they might leverage more positive change through a network of house-churches or apartment-churches than by capital investments in twenty-five acres of prime property.

To be sure, the expectations of the public for the church are unrealistic. That issue will be explored more fully in the next chapter. The point is that if public expectations are unrealistic, church organizations promise much and fail to deliver. They talk about changed lives, but seem to baptize a lot of babies for families who later disappear. They celebrate speaking in tongues, but can't seem to speak the language of their next-door neighbor. They tell stories of social transformation, but whatever transformations are happening do not seem to affect the nightly news. If all the people the church claims to be converting have really been converted, and if all the social advocacy and service the church claims to be doing really matter, then why isn't the world any different? Could it be because nobody really cares what the church says or does?

Even if the output of the church were relatively benign, people might still be willing to involve themselves in the organization. Some might be willing to be manipulated into supporting an organization that at least produces some good potluck suppers, quality amateur concerts, and pleasant fellowship, without making too many demands beyond the gifts of some time, talent, and money. Those who do enjoy home cooking, non-pop music, and generic coffee and conversation, and who are predisposed to appreciate antiques, might continue to support the church. The trouble is that it is increasingly clear that the output of the church is *not* benign. It is abusive.

Like gasoline engines, the traditional church organization leaves behind a waste product. It is a trail of used up, burned-out, disaffected, disillusioned, and often embittered people who have dropped out or moved to the margins of congregational life. They may not be vocally angry at the church. They are just not interested anymore. If they are vocally angry at the church, it is because, however noble or ignoble their personal aspirations, they feel they have lost the power struggle that is at the heart of traditional ecclesiastical life.

And a power struggle it is. Parliamentary procedure may make the struggle more polite, but it is a power struggle nonetheless. The more diverse society becomes, the more politicized church life becomes. Since a new generation (with a new fashion sense, a new musical taste, a new network of intimacy, and a new set of causes) emerges every three years, the power struggle becomes intense. Youth representatives on the boards and racial minorities on the committees won't blend incompatible agendas in a society in which seventeen-year-olds have no understanding whatsoever of thirteen-year-olds, and "tribes" are defined by tattoo and technology.

The basic idea in traditional church organizations is that if you wish to achieve your agenda (establish your music as dominant in worship, prioritize the budget to meet your goals, deploy staff to address your needs), then you need to elect (or appoint) your allies to office. Matriarchs and patriarchs extend their patronage toward selected newcomers who best reflect their set of personal values and private perspectives. Members of church groups lobby for their candidates to hold key offices or sit in key committees in the church. As the pool of volunteers shrinks, and the dependency on professionals grows, the key positions are on the finance committee, personnel committee, or board of trustees. If one loses the struggle here, one has only to win the struggle to control the next level of management.

In the end, it is the instability of power, and not any particular victory or defeat that fractures the fragile harmony of the church organization. Even megachurches are not immune. The beloved pastor will not live forever, and which congregational or denominational power bloc will succeed in replacing him or her? The current in-group of authority is already feeling weary of constant administration, and members' ability to find "suitable" replacements is increasingly doubtful. The victors today will likely be victims tomorrow. The satisfaction and contentment any particular group experiences at any particular time are not likely to last.

There *are* other organizational models. Non-bureaucratic and non-hierarchical models that are team-based, streamlined, and servant empowering are emerging in all sectors of society (corporate, nonprofit, social service, health care, even the military). These organizations are entrepreneurial, focused on adaptation and training, and are shaped bottom-up by the forces of changing culture. They are driving for results, questing for quality, and giving of permission. If they tend to be high-risk, they also tend to have high-impact. I have written about these organizations in my book *Christian Chaos* (Nashville: Abingdon, 1999). Some churches can change and are changing their organizational models, but not many.

Why? In the end, the cult of harmony holds traditional church organizations in a grasp that will not let go. The mythical lure of harmony is like the scent of alcohol to the nostrils of an alcoholic. Traditional organizations are designed to pursue the Holy Grail to be "one happy family," recapturing the supposed unity of the culturally homogeneous village church with the white steeple on top. Even though the community is more diverse, the church insists on only one worship service. Even though the volunteer pool is shrinking, it multiplies committees. It is convinced that harmony can be achieved if people would just sit in the same room, eat at the same table, and find their place in institutional management.

Tactics such as these are like pouring water on Greek Fire. It seems logical to the addicted leadership that if people are discontented, or if factions are fighting with one another, or if church dropouts are moving to the margins of congregational life, then more nurture will solve the problem.

- Get everybody to take personality inventories!
- Multiply fellowship opportunities!
- Expand the consensus management process!

Yet such tactics actually increase the flames, because no matter how much nurture you give the congregation, the ideal harmony is never achieved, and the frustration of the cult just grows and grows. Eventually the vicious circle of shrinking participation and expanding bureaucracy must lead to collapse, and that moment is coming perilously close.

## The Beleaguered Chaplaincy

At second glance, the fragility of the organization has nothing to do with structure, but everything to do with leadership. There are plenty of examples of traditional churches that have every structural or organizational advantage (money, location, facility, volunteers, mission statements, and the blessing of the bishop), and yet languish with stagnant worship attendance, bickering over trivialities, and low mission impact. There is a growing number of nontraditional, disadvantaged churches that seem to find a way to grow despite all odds. Their high impact on local and global mission is facilitated by nonordained, noncertified, noncharismatic leaders now on their second or third career path.

The trouble is that denominations and independent churches alike have not found a way to intentionally and predictably multiply this new species of leader. They are not enrolling in seminary, and if they do they frequently drop out. Those leaders who are growing churches today seem to emerge from the cultural wilderness at the whim of the Spirit, or they are transformed from within the traditional ranks of pastors by the unexpected intervention of a Higher Power at the point of deepest clergy despair. This, of course, would be reason to celebrate, if it were not for the fact that neither these leaders nor the church as a whole can find a way to intentionally and predictably support and network these leaders long term.

The fragility of the church today is not due to a lack of periodic brilliance in leadership, but rather to the lack of consistency in supporting brilliant leaders and multiplying their abilities.

- A credible, talented pastor may grow a church (in every sense of the "pediatric" metaphor of "growth") to increase participation, deepen spirituality, and multiply mission, and then retire, move on to another church, or burn out. Not only do churches consistently fail to understand *why* this happens to their clergy leaders, they consistently fail to replace them effectively. Judicatory and congregational assessment and placement procedures are evermore detailed and complex, and consistently fail to locate a successor who can continue the positive momentum.
- A passionate, skilled volunteer may guide a church board or mission team (in every sense of the "coaching" metaphor of leadership) to increase quality, articulate faith, and implement beneficial services, and then resign, relocate to another community, or drift to the margins of congregational life. Once again congregations consistently fail to understand *why* this

phenomenon happens, and even the most sophisticated nominations and appointment processes cannot replace them.

The church is like an aging golf pro who can still hit brilliant shots on the fairway, but can't seem to put two or three great shots together in a row. Or, stated another way, the church is like a baseball team that regularly loads the bases, but can't seem to get the clutch hits to drive someone home.

Why can't the church consistently deploy brilliant leaders? Because the church does not really *want* to deploy brilliant leaders. It prefers to deploy manageable chaplains. Brilliant leaders are by nature entrepreneurs. They experiment, they risk, they intuit unknown possibilities, they innovate unique strategies, they invent brand-new resources, and they "draw outside of the box." Brilliant leaders are focused on mission, refusing to be shackled by the institutional demands of a denomination or the privileged expectations of membership. The church (in all its manifestations as congregations, denominations, or theological colleges) prefers to inculcate and encourage dependency. It prefers manageable, tractable, obedient leaders, dependent on the institution, who are capable of making people dependent on them. These churches look for clergy and lay leaders who:

- replicate denominational programs;
- implement uniform liturgy;
- develop hierarchical staff;
- rely on publishing house resources;
- synchronize congregational goals with denominational strategic planning;
- anticipate nontaxable benefits and retirement pensions.

Dependency ultimately leads to mediocrity. It is a kind of spiritual and institutional inbreeding that results in much professional collegiality, but little daring creativity. And the church prefers it that way.

Seminary enrollment is diminishing, but not because the public is any less interested in forming partnerships to explore spiritual things or to do faith-based activities. Part of the lack of interest in church leadership is due to the wasteful organizational models in which the church expects leaders to function. However, decreasing seminary enrollment is also due to the intransigent demand of the church institution for harmonious, manageable, institutional players. Don't just lament who is *not* in seminary. Examine who *is,* and what happens to them.

- First, there are seekers. This fastest growing group is made up of earnest inquirers and spiritual dilettantes who are simply trying to gain a deeper, broader spiritual perspective on their own lives and lifestyles. They have no real intention to lead a congregation, and do not last long if they do.
- Second, there are students of religion. This group emphasizes the foundational disciplines of biblical studies, history, and theology—often with a contextual perspective and sociological methodology—and intends to teach or do expository preaching. The dearth of great preaching pulpits and the difficulty in gaining senior pastor status soon send these folks to alternate academic or public school careers.
- Third, there are spiritual entrepreneurs seeking legitimacy. These are creative risk-takers, often prepared to explore innovative congregational ministries, but hoping that the degree and subsequent credentials will open doors and provide some security for themselves and their families. They may stay long term with their first congregations, but are often considered fringe to the seminary and mavericks to the judicatory. When things get rough, they may shift to a parachurch or faith-based nonprofit agency.
- Fourth, there are favored children. These are the people recommended by their congregations, raised by their judicatories, motivated by Christendom. They

have synchronized academic and polity training. They
may count several uncles and grandparents among the
clergy. They have great appreciation for historic and
institutional continuity. They go far in their clergy
careers, but increasing numbers of them are going on
disability because the stress of maintaining the cult of
harmony becomes intolerable.

Of course, there are exceptions to all four generalizations. Some
seekers eventually become passionate Christian disciples and congregational leaders, but they are always disruptively outside the
denominational ethos. Some spiritual entrepreneurs do lead long-
term innovative congregational ministries, but they refuse episco-
pal appointments and decline to follow the professional career
ladder. Some students of religion do lead spiritually deep congregations, but their sense of integrity resists ecclesiastical compro-
mise, or their commitment to ideology challenges church policy,
or their passion for context appreciates divergent cultures and traditions. Some favored children do grow stable church organizations, but are drawn into the vortex of managing financial crisis,
personnel litigation, and marketing to a hostile public—and away
from congregational ministry. Most of these seminary students are
ultimately driven out by the cult of harmony embraced by the
church. They either do not want any part of the codependency of
the church, or they embrace it and are destroyed by it.

What about volunteer leadership? Volunteerism, like charitable
giving, is up everywhere in North America. This is true *despite* the
fact that life is busier than ever. Yet when people are asked to volunteer for the church, the most common answer is "I don't have
time." Surely part of this lack of enthusiasm is due to the wasteful organizational models that can no longer compete with better-
organized charities, social services, and parachurches that do not
waste time. However, decreasing church volunteerism is also due
to the demand for obedience to an institution coupled with an
expectation for membership privileges. Don't lament who is *not*
volunteering. Examine who *is*, and what happens to them.

- First, there are seekers. This is a large, but hidden group who usually camouflage their spiritual yearning by requesting infant baptism or friendly fellowship with Christians. They respond well to time/talent stewardship programs, but drop out quickly once they discover the church is more interested in their talent than their "abundant life."
- Second, there are teenagers and membership transfers. Both groups volunteer as a means of penetrating into the heart of the fellowship, which means that they are more interested in attending meetings about mission than actually doing it. Teens volunteer to teach Sunday school in order to flee boring worship, and newly received members volunteer for offices as a way of making influential friends. Unlike their parents who transferred membership to other churches, the teens who drop out rarely return even when they are married. Weary and secretly bored, the "transfers" eventually distance themselves from the board and invest in the supper club.
- Third, there are parents with children in school (K-12). Since the cult of harmony celebrates the "family church," it is no surprise that many of the volunteers are parents with children still at home. They and the church know that if the kids are to receive any Christian education at all, or any incentive to appreciate corporate worship and cultural heritage, these parents will have to do it. Once the kids are gone, however, they are apt to stop volunteering because they have "done their bit" and it is time for others to do theirs.
- Fourth, there are women over the age of forty-five. This group has been the mainstay of church volunteerism for three decades. They lead and attend the dwindling adult Sunday school classes. They chair and participate in most of the committees. They care more passionately about the faithfulness of the church, and the future of the world, than most of the men on the finance committee, and therefore are responsible for raising the money for the church budget. Yet even this group is shrinking. Some are dying; many are burned-out from the workload; still more are angry that

they do all the work and a few aging males set all the policy; and very many have discovered that the church is no longer the only way, or even the best way, in which one can live a meaningful life.

Of course, there are exceptions. Some seekers do find that "churchy" environments feed their souls. Some teenagers do come back, and some "transfers" become passionate about hands-on mission and spiritual growth. Some parents (men and women) continue their board and committee leadership after the kids have left home. Some women over the age of forty-five remain loyal to the denomination, and yes, some men stay involved and even share power with women. That small percentage of volunteers who embrace the cult of harmony eventually discard the church when it no longer directly addresses their personal needs, or drop out because the idyllic promise of meaningful life was never fulfilled.

Demographers in both the United States and Canada agree, however, that the most likely person to volunteer for anything in North America will be a married female over the age of forty-five, of northern European descent, with a family income over U.S.$40,000 or Can$60,000, who lives or has roots in a midsized, midwest town. That person is now dropping out of the traditional, institutional church. Not only can the church not recapture that person's interest, it can't build a consistent leadership pool from a different demographic.

Why? Why are the best and brightest leaders (clergy and laity) dropping out of the institutional church? And why can't the church tap the huge volunteer movement in North America to revitalize and multiply its own leadership pool?

The answer is that the cult of harmony (which traps church organization) has generated an obsession with chaplaincy (which sidetracks and eventually disables church leadership). Here is the predicament:

- The institution asks, "You love the church, don't you?"

- The membership responds, "How dare you ask me to do what we pay professionals to accomplish better."
- The clergy despairs, "People are so diverse, so busy, and so needy, and we just can't take care of everybody anymore!"
- The seminary declares, "Just do more continuing education and we'll help you run faster and do more!"
- The motivated, spiritually growing lay leaders complain, "Why can't institutions, clergy, and members let us be ministers?"

The cult of harmony causes the institution to manufacture evermore hoops and hurdles with which volunteers must be "certified" to be obedient, manageable institutional players. It causes the traditional membership to resist and resent the ministry offered by their peers, lest one layperson's excellence in ministry judge another layperson's mediocrity in participation. It causes the clergy to worry about their job security and central importance to the church family. It causes both clergy and laity primarily concerned with mission to leave. When they do, the institution declares with mingled hurt and anger, "We thought you loved the church!"

We see again the "Greek Fire phenomenon." In an effort to quench the fires of discontent, the church pours onto the flames more propaganda about denominational loyalty, the membership pours on higher expectations for ministry professionalism, and the clergy pours on more pressure for higher salaries and pension benefits. These efforts do not achieve the mythic harmony that is the selective historical memory of the church. In fact, these efforts render the denomination even less credible, broaden the gap between clergy and laity even more, and accelerate clergy burnout, disability, and career change.

The effect of the cult of harmony on leadership is that it transforms congregational leaders into institutional chaplains. The congregation attracts needy people who perceive themselves to be relatively helpless people. The congregational ministry attracts leaders who have a need to be needed, who perceive themselves to be relatively competent caregivers. Those laity who are *not* needy and helpless either leave the church, or don the uniform of a spiritual "nurse" in order to take care of the rest of the spiritual hospice. Those clergy who are not competent caregivers either leave the pastorate or don the uniform of a spiritual "doctor" and try to enjoy constant home and institutional visitation.

Both membership and clergy will likely bridle at being labeled in this way. The laity are *not* simply needy and helpless, and the clergy are *not* simply taking care of people to feed their self-esteem. Yet that is the point. They are *not* supposed to be like this, but *that is exactly how they behave.*

- Most of the budget is given over to staff salaries and benefits.
- Most of the laity do little more than raise money to pay others to do ministry.
- Almost no money is spent on the continuing education of volunteers.
- Little happens unless paid staff initiate it, teach it, lead it, advocate it, and ultimately implement it.
- Clergy visit, visit, and visit more, while laity constantly complain they are not visited enough.
- Nothing happens until the new minister comes, and when the new minister comes he or she reasonably expects to change everything to suit his or her purposes.

No matter what the rhetoric might be about the priesthood of all believers, the church still behaves like there is just one priest. No matter how many programs the church implements, it still relies on salaried staff to plan, implement, supervise, and evaluate them. All the effort to discover personality profiles is really aimed at helping church insiders get along better, and all the time spent discerning spiritual gifts is really designed to implement the clergy's agenda, and all the money raised for "ministries" is really spent on salaries, properties, and the music that church insiders love best.

Chaplaincy is not just about visitation. It is really about feeding the self-centeredness of the congregation. The cult of harmony has made the traditional Christian congregation one of the most selfish organizations in North America. It's all "me, me, me, me!" It's about *my* church, *my* music, *my* technological preferences, *my* ideological priorities, *my* physical and mental infirmities, *my* mission agenda, *my* money, *my* pastor, and *my* flock. It's about taking care of my needs and desires *first*, and if there is any staff energy, volunteer time, or budgeted money left over after *my* personal and institutional needs are met, we'll give it away to others. This is the dark side, the cultic side, of the church's obsession with harmony. It extends beyond the congregation to the regional judicatory and the national denomination.

- The congregation nurtures leaders to feed it.
- The seminary trains leaders to feed it.
- The judicatory deploys leaders to feed it.
- The leaders who have been nurtured, trained, and deployed in that codependent environment enjoy it too much to give it up.
- Any leader who refuses to feed the essential selfishness of the church is forced out, or must endure enormous conflict in order to free the congregation for mission.

Chaplaincy is all about feeding the cult of harmony. They'll know we are Christians by our love, all right, but it's the internal love congregational members, judicatory representatives, denominational offices, and seminary alumni have for one another, not the love they have for mission in God's world. Ironically, one of the most common criticisms of any form of outreach (worship, mission projects, and evangelism) and any form of welcoming ministry (indigenous worship, visitor friendly facilities, refreshments) is that it "puts us out." Imagine! Traditional churches accuse *the public* of being selfish! Claiming to be inclusive, the church becomes the most exclusive club in the community. They only open certain hours, do things certain ways, fund certain projects, and enroll certain people. And they expect the clergy to keep it that way.

## The Inadequate Continuum

At third glance, the fragility of the organization has nothing to do with either structure or leadership, but everything to do with their perception of reality. The church desperately wants to separate reality into the "sacred" and the "secular," so that it can control that half of reality that has to do with the "sacred." It is preoccupied with sacred space (location, architecture, and floor plan), sacred time (the Christian year), and sacred people (the clergy). The more endangered this perception of divided reality becomes, the more desperately the church labors to control these things.

- The preoccupation with sacred space drives churches to pool capital for property development, spend huge amounts of money for architecture and technology that have little market value, standardize interior design, preserve sacred sacramental objects, and burden church planters with capital debts. If any congregation disturbs the harmony of the church too much, the denomination can always foreclose or withhold subsidies.
- The preoccupation with sacred time drives churches to design curriculum and worship around a calendar nobody uses, intrude condescendingly or judgmentally on the work and play of the week, and focus staff energies on the key life-cycle moments of birth, marriage, and death. If any clergy or lay leaders disturb the harmony of the church too much, members can always complain to the receptive ears of judicatory investigators eager for every denominational franchise to worship alike, and every franchise manager to nurture the

young, reconcile interpersonal relationships, and visit the sick.

- The preoccupation with sacred people drives churches to multiply the requirements of ordination, restrict the opportunities of lay ministers, increase the use of vestments and albs and obscure terminology in worship, protect pension benefits, and supervise clergy constantly. Misconduct among clergy becomes more heinous than parallel misconduct among ordinary people, and preaching by clergy becomes more exalted than parallel speeches made by ordinary people. If any clergy disturb the harmony of the church too much, they can be removed from office, counseled by their clergy peers, or encouraged to take continuing education at the seminary where they will be set on the right path.

The church is more interested in controlling these three aspects of the sacred than in understanding or conversing with the other half of its reality. By preserving the legitimacy of these three aspects of the sacred, the cult of harmony tries to maintain a perception of divided reality that is being assaulted from every sector of human endeavor.

And that perception of reality is under assault! Healthcare is becoming more holistic, education is exploring the metaphysical and cultural underpinnings of ethics, science is talking about God, business is embedding core ideology and behavior, social services are becoming faith-based, politicians have recognized religion as a legitimate force, and mystery and myth pervade twenty-first-century media. More than this, faith and lifestyle have merged; work and leisure have united in a seamless experience; peer groups have replaced families as the organizational units of society; social justice, environmental purity, and higher consciousness all overlap in the transformational vision of the public; and the destiny of humanity, the destiny of the planet, and the will of the divine are relevant topics to the most materialistic advertising campaigns. The secular world is gone. It has been replaced by a world of "spirits" and many "gods."

On the one hand, the effort to separate a "sacred" from a "secular" world is treated by the twenty-first-century public as amusing and anachronistic. It is a relatively harmless activity, but the public will not rezone subdivisions to allow for sacred space, reschedule Little League games to respect sacred time, nor extend tax exemptions to discriminate in favor of sacred people. On the other hand, the effort to control a sacred continuum is regarded by the public as suspiciously demonic. It is demonic not just because it leads to judgment and confrontation in a world of multiple cultures, but because it tries to control what is essentially uncontrollable, limit what is essentially universal, and rationalize what is essentially mysterious.

The cult of harmony positions itself over against the holistic experience of the world. "*We* experience true peace, quality intimacy, gender equality, cross-cultural respect, and healthy relationships, but *they* do not. If only those people would join our circle, they could be rescued from their violence, brokenness, sexism, racism, and unhealthy lives." The trouble, of course, is that most observers can see that people inside the church actually experience less peace, intimacy, equality, respect, and health than people outside of the church. Most do see that, unless they are members of the cult.

Harmony, of course, is a good thing, but the modern church has warped the experience into a cult. In the same way love is a good thing, but dysfunctional people warp the experience into a codependency. And in the same way, institutional chaplaincy is a good thing, but cultic obsession with harmony imposes it as the standard of congregational life. The "cult" of harmony is no mere metaphor for the way "church" is commonly practiced in both its liberal and conservative congregational and denominational forms. It is "cultic."

- It is ritualistic in every way, from passing the peace in Sunday worship, to passing the coffee in post-service refreshments, to telephone trees to pray for the sick.

- It is sectarian (exclusive of other subcultures), unorthodox (foreign to the contextual spirituality of diverse publics in the community), and antisocial (causing more people to kill each other, argue with each other, or divorce each other than any other organization).
- It is devoted to things (pews, property, organs, and memorials), and it does homage to certain people (clergy, matriarchs, trustees, bishops, and dead saints whose names are inscribed on brass plaques and stained-glass windows).
- It is a fashion followed by a specific section of society, in which people share common aesthetic tastes, transportation preferences, and economic choices.
- It is popularized and marketed to give prescriptive advice on right living and personal guarantees for salvation, and the people who take that advice seriously and believe in those guarantees do assemble regularly and love one another very much.

The fragility of the organization is due partly to the fact that the public sees the church as a cult, not as a healthy organization. The perception of reality among cult leaders that separates the "sacred" and the "secular" encourages this public perception. Not many people want to join a cult. The fragility of the organization is also due, however, to the fact that the church is just one cult among many competitors in the religion market today. It competes as such not only with the mosque and the synagogue, but also with IBM, eBay, the United Way, and the local softball league. These latter organizations have become as spiritually compelling as the former organizations have become pragmatically businesslike. The church, now going the way of the dinosaurs and dime stores, just does not understand the competition today.

The cult of harmony has been developed around the perception that divides reality between the "sacred" and the "secular," and its strategic plan developed to control that half which is "sacred." That is why the conflicts that most seriously rock the church are usually about property change, liturgical practice, and personnel deployment. That is why denominational staff, budget, and energy are deployed around financial subsidies, worship and curriculum standardization, and personnel certification. Just manage those things well and harmony will reign in the church!

That is also why an increasingly amused and suspicious public steps up its assault on the inadequate perceived reality of the traditional church. This is not a conspiracy. It is simply a wellspring of frustration with an organization that may have much to say about eternal truth, but which is so enthralled by its own cultic trappings that it cannot seem to help people connect with eternity. It is no accident that public scrutiny, controversy, and litigation concentrates on the very same three things the church tries so mightily to control. Just destabilize church control over these three things, force the church beyond its inadequate perceptions of reality, and the entire organization will collapse!

| | **Stress from Within** | **Stress from Beyond** |
|---|---|---|
| **Sacred Space** | Obsession with worship space, sacred objects, and heritage symbols diversifies so rapidly that churches split over the smallest changes. | Property tax exemptions, parking privileges, rental discounts of public facilities, zoning leniency, airspace rights, advertisement loopholes for signage all disappear. |
| **Sacred Time** | Obsession with Sunday mornings, quarrels over liturgy and scheduling, struggles to define "active" and "inactive" membership dominate board agendas and disgruntle church dropouts. | Shopping and sports usurp Sunday morning, cultural holidays dominate school calendars, spiritual consumers seek convenience, noise bylaws silence church bells and carillons, cell phones go off in funerals and weddings. |

| | Stress from Within | Stress from Beyond |
|---|---|---|
| **Sacred People** | Obsession with clergy privileges, disillusionment with clergy shortcomings, power struggle over church offices, and politicizing of the career ladder overwhelm leaders with conflict, bureaucracy, and trivial administration. | Civil litigation against clergy escalates, disability and health insurance break judicatory budgets, religious leaders are stereotyped and ridiculed in the media, police screen Sunday school teachers, and church leaders are scrutinized by the IRS. |

The more "cultic" the harmony of the church becomes, the more stress points fracture the harmony, and the more fragile the harmony becomes. Yet as the internal and external stresses threaten the fragile harmony of the church, the reaction of the church is to try even more vigorously to control the "sacred territory" of space, time, and people.

- Internally, churches do more personality inventories, publish more architectural manuals, hymnbooks, and liturgical guidelines, add more requirements to candidacy for ordination, hire more judicatory personnel officers, and contract with more conflict resolution consultants.
- Externally, churches invest in more land-banking, petition city hall to protect Sundays, protest the board of education, hire more lawyers, buy off complainants with more capital funds, create right- or left-wing political parties to counter public policy, and decry the media.

In and of themselves, such strategies can protect the rights of any organization. However, given the context of the cult of harmony, and the related addiction to "chaplaincy" leadership, such tactics simply throw water onto Greek Fire.

This is the desperate situation of the church at the start of the twenty-first century. Fewer people find the church relevant to their spiritual and social context (especially people under the age of forty-five, especially women and people of alternate lifestyles, especially people of non-Western or northern-European descent, especially people for whom English is not an indigenous language, especially seniors bored with six decades of churchy behavior). Why? Because the structures and programs used to address the holistic yearnings of the public are no longer working. Why? Because the leaders who design, implement, and monitor these structures and programs have been entrapped by codependencies based on pastoral care and membership privileges. Why? Because these leaders are obsessed by a perception of reality that is too limited for a world of speed, flux, and blur, a world in which real time and virtual time have merged.

Despite the appearance of health, churches at the turn of the millennium are more fragile and more vulnerable than ever before. The cult of harmony has forged chains of chaplaincy, shackling church leaders to a limited perception of reality. Even the healthiest churches may be just one pastoral relationship, just one core member's death, just one ideological conflict, just one natural disaster, or just one program fiasco away from amalgamation and closure. The decline that used to take decades can now be measured in months.

## Why Is It So Hard to Plant New Churches?

Traditional church planting among the denominations of North America has been the responsibility of the middle or national judicatory. They collected the capital pool to finance the project, completed the demographic research to locate the new church, interviewed the candidate to be deployed to start the new congregation, supervised the progress to make sure the new church represented faithfully the denominational ethos, subsidized the new congregation until it could finance its own budget, and cer-

tified both organizational model and staff. The goal was to replicate the denominational franchise across the country so exactly
that one could literally walk into any church and feel right at
home. New church development represented the cult of harmony
in an expansionist form.

It worked well so long as the public was generally homogeneous, and interested solely in choosing which Christian franchise it wanted to join. It worked well so long as the fledgling new
church could easily harvest the demographic growth. Today the
public is diverse. The choice to join a Christian faith community
is the least popular option among a panoply of pagan "gods."
Fewer people are attracted to a cult of harmony because their real
desire is to find hope. They want one good reason not to commit
suicide tonight, and if they need to be disharmonized to experience it, that's fine. The harmony of the denominational church
franchise has become an obstacle to their spiritual quest.

Fewer than 10 percent of newly planted churches grow much
beyond 125 members or 250 worshipers after ten years. A significant number of newly planted churches fail after five years,
unable to attract new members or achieve financial stability.
Denominational personnel support and financial subsidy may
keep them alive for as much as another decade, but they never
really grow. Why? Because despite the theoretical commitment to
outreach, they are really committed to harmony. They gather people uncomfortable with the aesthetics of a traditional church, who
then create a new aesthetic unity that is comfortable for them.
From the very beginning, the church was never really about mission, but about membership. It was never really about hope, but
about harmony.

Most new church developments are therefore founded on
polity, program, and membership privileges. Denominational
polity demands bureaucratic and hierarchical organizational
models that are increasingly foreign to the lives of laity, but which
are designed to impose uniformity. Congregational mission is
shaped around gender and generational programs that are
increasingly foreign to affinity-oriented, cross-cultural people.
Membership privileges build congregational unity around

aesthetic taste, appearance, and sensibility. That may mean contemporary music, gymnasium architecture, and cooperative social service, or it may mean traditional music, classic steeple and pews, and cooperative program maintenance, but it still means that "our kind of people will do whatever it takes to live in harmony here."

Jim Griffith is one of North America's foremost cross-denominational coaches for church planters, and an associate with Easum, Bandy & Associates. He identifies five character traits for effective church planting leadership:

| | | |
|---|---|---|
| 1. *Tenacity* | The concentration never to look back, turn back, or give up. |
| 2. *Generosity* | The willingness to give away just about anything to succeed. |
| 3. *Drivenness* | The passion to compete, achieve, and succeed. |
| 4. *Centered spirituality* | The serenity to experience God in the midst of brokenness. |
| 5. *Constant adaptability* | The freedom to change tactics, revise plans, and rethink principles. |

The fact is that the cult of harmony leaves the leadership and organization of a fledgling church in a very precarious position, because these five character traits that are valued highly in the world are precisely what denominational leaders do not highly value in a new church. Leaders who possess these character traits are hard to find.

First, modern denominations and traditional congregations do not raise or train leaders with these characteristics. These characteristics do not readily emerge from the culture of modern congregational life (even though they once did in previous centuries). Leaders are not readily trained by modern seminaries and theological colleges (even though they once were in previous centuries).

- Modern denominations prefer "reasonableness" to "tenacity." The want even their church planters to constantly "look back" and replicate denominational ethos. They want their church planters to divert their attention to denominational issues.

- Modern denominations prefer "responsible self-interest" to radical "generosity." They expect church planters to rely on minimum salaries and pension plans, pursue the career ladder, and reflect the lifestyle standards and norms of other salaried clergy.
- Modern denominations prefer "professionalism" to "drivenness." They ask church planters to measure success by quality of community life rather than by extent of mission outreach, and prize tidy record keeping and balanced budgets over risk.
- Modern denominations prefer "ideological correctness" to "centered spirituality." They want church planters to advocate the proper public policy, teach authorized curriculum, preach eternal dogma, or model "good" worship.
- Modern denominations prefer "predictable continuity" to "constant adaptability." They want church planters to be faithful to a heritage rather than to a mission, implement only approved strategic plans, and approach cultural diversity with suspicion.

These expectations may not be explicit. Individual denominational leaders may even deny them. However, they are a part of the hidden, dominant, corporate culture of the modern church. Seek as they will, denominations find it hard to recruit church planters. Try as they might to be accepted, church planters feel at odds with their parent denominations.

However, the situation of new church development is even more precarious. Not only do church planters feel increasingly uncomfortable with their parent denominations, but they often come to feel increasingly uncomfortable with their own congregations! The pattern persists. The leader who plants a church leaves within a decade of the congregation's formation. The true, hidden purpose of the new congregation for cultic harmony finally emerges. No matter how beloved the original leader might be, as the congregation "matures" they all realize that they do not really want a leader who is tenacious, radically generous, driven to achieve, spiritually centered, or constantly adaptable! They want what the denomination wants: a leader who is reasonable, cautious, professional, correct, and predictable. Even among new church developments, in the end it's about harmony for the few and not hope for the masses.

There are exceptions, of course. There are newly planted churches that not only grow quickly, but continue growing year after year. They multiply indigenous worship options, spiritual growth alternatives, and local or global mission teams. Demographic limitations and the increasing unpopularity of religious institutions in the pagan world of North America may limit their individual increase, but not their multiplication of cells. Denominational authorities and established congregations may view these churches suspiciously, but they are the future of mission in North America.

The mentors and models for many of these successful church plants have not been denominational parents from within North America, but congregational partners from beyond North America. A recent article in the *Journal for the Scientific Study of Religion* confirmed what, for these congregations, has become a common assumption, namely, that the more pluralistic a community becomes the less likely people are to join religious organizations (Daniel V. A. Olson and C. Kirk Hadaway, "Religious Pluralism and Affiliation Among Canadian Counties and Cities," vol. 38, no. 4 [December 1999], pp. 490-508). The tactic to grow a church through harmony based on taste, appearance, and sensibility won't work. The community niche of uniformity will not only be too small, but organizations of any kind that do not truly reflect diversity are not credible to the cross-cultural public.

For years denominations and established congregations have worried that new church developments might "accommodate to culture" by adopting alternative tactics of worship, spiritual growth, and outreach. Successful church plants force the church to face an unpleasant truth. The established church long ago accommodated to culture, and now newly planted churches must do all in their power to liberate the church to be faithful once again. The challenge today is not to keep the gospel pure from cultural accommodation, but to disentangle the authentic gospel from centuries of accommodation to western European culture.

These exceptional new churches, mentored from beyond North America, represent the hope that the fragile organization that is the church today can indeed be reformed, redirected, and renewed. If it is true that the cult of harmony has forged chains of chaplaincy, which shackle church participants to a limited perception of reality, then (to paraphrase Paul in Rom. 7:24), "Who is to rescue us from this cycle of death?" Church planting, inspired by models beyond North America, can provide the answer.

Some clues are already visible in the international context, as a new species of church emerges in cultural chaos. Robin Trebilcock tells the story of Prospect Road Uniting Church in Adelaide, South Australia. (See the Easum, Bandy & Associates Web site for the complete article entitled "Community on the OtherSide—Some Clues to Post-Modern Church" [http://www.easumbandy.com/members/articles/community_on_the_otherside.html], which is available by becoming a member of the EBA community.)

This congregation (like so many of the new species of emerging church) is clearly shaped around congregationally defined core values, leadership multiplication, and mission urgency, rather than polity, program, and membership privileges. Three distinct demographic groupings replaced five distinct church buildings as the key to mission. Each demographic grouping in turn shaped for itself the style of worship, learning methodologies, and programs of service that were most helpful and relevant for their context. They considered carefully how people process their life information and experience, establishing ministries for head (people who value cognitive process), heart (people who value relationships and image), and gut (people who value feelings and experimentation). Each community practices an open-range philosophy that allows the public to come and go at the pace of their daily lifestyles, rather than the dictates of a Christian year.

Trebilcock describes a different kind of connectivity in this church that resembles an organic body more than an ecclesiastical machine. The modern "traditional" church, he says, is hard wired. People are connected by rules, controls, sanctions, loyalties, and expectations of privilege. The fullness of the gospel can only be realized through consistent participation over an extended period of time. In contrast, this church enjoys a "synaptic connectivity" like an organic brain. Just as electrons leap over gaps from cell to cell, so also the spiritual yearning of the seeking public allows them to leap from experience to experience as unpredictable opportunity arises. The key is not to rely on cumulative experience to communicate the fullness of the gospel, but to make each synaptic event an experience of the fullness of the gospel. Community is formed by the immediacy of individual encounters with the Holy, not the regularity of attendance in an institution.

In what may be peculiarly Australian mixed metaphors, Trebilcock describes leadership as a kind of constant "walk about." The "sheep" are not contained in a pen, but allowed to wander the open range of culture. The entrepreneurial leader "walks about," paying attention to changing patterns to the ecosystem of culture, intervening as circumstances require, managing the system but generally keeping out of the way of the sheep. There are four styles of worship (classic, discussion, parent/child, and "soul café"), and people choose whatever works best for them. The skeptical, alienated, fearful, yearning public is drawn into a relationship with Christ that influences daily lifestyle, rather than to membership in an institution that merely affects charitable giving.

The attitude of a traditional, denominationally planted new church toward discontented people is much the same as an established denominational franchise. If you are discontented, join a committee, make friends with the right people, or leave to find a place where you can enjoy harmony. But the attitude of this new species of church is quite different.

- *If you are discontented, you may have a vision we need to see.* The creativity and spiritual growth of participants shapes and reshapes the organization.

- *If you are discontented, you may have a different gift we need to nurture.* The individual does not exist to serve the organization, but the organization exists to serve the individual.
- *If you are discontented, you deserve a better spiritual guide.* The best way to serve individuals is not to make them dependent on professional help, but to guide them to help themselves and others.

Broaden the sensitivity to culture. Liberate entrepreneurial leaders to do whatever unexpected things are required. Enable the public to experience the fullness of the Holy in the course and timing of *their* lifestyles. In the end, you no longer have a cult of harmony. You have a matrix of hope.

Greek Fire loses its mystery and terror when you understand that its power lies not in the fire itself, but in the vulnerabilities of a church organization that is no longer compatible with culture. You don't fight this fire with water (more personnel officers, more ad hoc investigative committees, more procedures). You fight this fire with fire.

You must fundamentally surrender the cult of harmony that is the hidden assumption of the modern traditional church. God never intended the church to be one happy family, but a bubbling cauldron of spiritual growth, mission experiment, and passionate desire to be with Jesus in the mission field. The ancient unity of the church had little to do with common economic, educational, or racial backgrounds, and it did not rely on shared aesthetic tastes or ideological interests. Their unity was a unity of *purpose.* They were united because they wanted to add their gifts, whatever they were, to the mission of Jesus in the world.

If you are fundamentally focused on harmony, good feeling, fellowship, and membership privilege, then Greek Fire will consume you in an instant in this changed cultural environment. The more you want to survive, the faster you will perish. It will happen despite all the personnel training, consciousness-raising, and procedures your denomination devises.

If you are fundamentally on fire to be with Jesus in the mission field, then fire will fight fire. The more united you are around purpose, the more diversity will feed your passion. Discontent will become a way of life, because there can be no real contentment until it is experienced with Jesus and creation returns to the original perfection of Eden.

# Three

## THE CONFUSED MISSIONARY

We all know what happens when an individual is deprived of the use of her five senses by external circumstances. She loses her sense of direction. A dense fog, intensely bright lights, constant surround-sound noise, toxic odors, and even the sudden inability to touch and feel the real world can be extraordinarily confusing. The previous chapter suggested that regaining sensitivity to the realities of contemporary diversity, the immediacy of Christ, and the urgency of mission could shatter the cult of harmony and liberate leaders to become the apostles God intends them to be. Over the centuries, many reformers and prophets have called to the church through the fog of circumstance, and helped the church regain clarity of purpose.

However, the situation of the contemporary North American church (and its counterparts in Europe and Australia) is more serious than this. The confusion is not just the result of external circumstances undermining the sensitivity of the church. It is actually the result of internal confusions that have impaired the five senses from perceiving reality rightly, even if that reality was as starkly clear as a sunny day in winter. The reformers and prophets of modern times are increasingly despairing. They have never been so clear, so precise, and so plain in their communication. Yet the church doggedly continues to run in circles around trivialities of ideology and dogma, or stands transfixed before the headlights of onrushing paganism. What more can they do?

The problem is internal, not external, to the body of Christ. It is not as if a healthy, normally acute person is lost in the fog, but rather an unhealthy, drug-dependent person is lost in the sunlight. The challenge is not to protect the integrity of the church from cacophony of cultural expectations, but to free the church from over fifteen hundred years of constant cultural accommodation. The "drug" has been in the veins of the body of Christ for a long time. It has driven the body of Christ in North America to oxygen tanks, crutches, and so many "drug rehabilitation" programs that the church has become dependent on them. The end result is that the church is profoundly, deeply, seriously confused about its mission.

The mission of the church is to multiply disciples of Jesus. That is its earliest mandate. That is what the apostles, the "road runners" of the Roman world, originally set out to do. The multiplication of disciples will affect personal peace and joy, as well as positive and even radical social change. The purpose, however, is neither personal joy nor social change as such. These are secondary, although desirable results. The purpose is to multiply disciples. After all, discipleship may not lead to either personal peace and joy or positive social change. Discipleship is a value unto itself.

The following parable has never failed to annoy traditional congregational leaders and veteran church people, so it is worth telling again:

> Once upon a time there was a cabdriver. He routinely picked people up at the airport and delivered them to their destinations in the city. He was a shrewd businessman. He believed in strategic planning.
>
> One day as he was waiting at the taxi stand, a man rushed out of the airport doors and into his cab. "Where to, buddy?" the cab driver asked.
>
> "Oh, just drive me around the block a few times, and return me to the airport terminal," came the reply.

Puzzled, the cabdriver asked, "What for?"

"Well, the fact is that in my busy life, rushing from place to place and city to city, I find taxi rides relaxing. They help me become more productive to fulfill my agenda. So just drive me around awhile, and when I feel refreshed, I can return for my next flight out of town."

Shrugging his shoulders, the cabdriver did as he was told. He returned his passenger to the terminal, and was given a fat tip for his efforts.

No sooner had the man left the cab than a woman rushed out of the terminal doors. "Where to, lady?"

"Oh, just drive me around the block a few times," came the reply.

Puzzled again, the driver asked, "What for?"

The woman smiled. "You see, I used to live in this area, and whenever I'm in town I like to just drive around and see the old neighborhood. It reminds me of my dear old mum."

Once again the taxi driver drove around the block a few times. He dropped the woman off at the terminal, and received a fat tip.

Now this same thing happened over and over again. The taxi driver was not stupid. He recognized an opportunity when he saw it. He bought another taxicab, and then another, until he had a whole fleet of taxicabs that would pick people up at the airport, drive them around the block a few times, and then return them to the terminal. The tips were out of this world.

Of course, the other cab drivers were not stupid either. Several other entrepreneurs also invested in more taxis, and soon there were whole fleets of taxis competing for the attention of people who enjoyed being driven around the block. As time passed, and times changed, the competition grew. Fewer and fewer people wanted to ride around the block. In order to keep going, our taxi driver did everything he could to make his taxis attractive.

The first thing he did was to take a class in public speaking. He trained himself to give the best verbal commentary to his customers as he drove them around the block. He knew every interesting detail about the neighborhood. He told the funniest jokes.

People would leave his cab laughing. "Boy, you were great!" they would say. "Next time I'm in town, I'll be sure to take your cab."

The second thing he did was to introduce great coffee. The refreshments served in his cab were first-class, the coffee fresh brewed, and he even provided juice for health-conscious adults and donuts for the kids.

The third thing he did was the most radical. He extended his cabs, and widened his cabs, to create a huge stage. Dancing girls would entertain his guests as they drove around the old neighborhood. Music, video, film—he had the best of everything.

However, despite all his strategic planning, ridership continued to diminish. Fewer and fewer people got into his cab. He watched the competition slowly disappear. He sold off one cab, then another, until finally, he was reduced to his one original taxicab. The bottom line was that fewer and fewer people wanted to just ride around the block and return to the place from which they started.

Of course, this is a parable of the modern traditional church on the brink of the twenty-first century. A process that had been happening for centuries was accelerated by world wars, mass migrations, and cultural diversity. The more mobile people became, the more they needed help to focus their personal plans and keep in touch with their roots. Sociologists have long observed that the church is one of the best social institutions to do both. Denominational leaders were aware of this opportunity, and franchised denominational churches multiplied on every urban corner and rural intersection. Busy people eager to be more productive six days a week, and rootless people eager to regain a sense of belonging flocked to the church. The church drove them around the Christian year, returning them to Advent and Christmas.

Unfortunately, "ridership" around the Christian year is falling off. People have found other ways to relax and focus their productive lives without the financial and dogmatic overhead of the church. People have found other ways to recognize their roots and build relationships (through amateur sports, recreation, and the Internet) without the organ music and committee meetings. Certainly there are still some people who like to ride in taxicabs, but most either own their own car or are taking other forms of spiritual transportation. As the competition increases, denominational franchises experiment:

- Leaders take continuing education courses in preaching and communication. They train themselves to give the best possible verbal commentary on the Christian year. They tell funny jokes and cute children's stories. People shake hands at the church door. "Boy, you were great!" they say. "Next time I feel like going to church, I'll be sure to come here!"
- Congregations introduce great coffee. Their refreshments are the best. Their potluck suppers are the talk of the town. And their receptions following every funeral are truly "to die for." The aroma of specialty coffee and cappuccino wafts through the sanctuary.
- Churches tear out the chancel, and enlarge the facility. They maximize entertainment, buy new choir robes, form an easy-listening band, and pick up the beat. They have the best video, film, and music in town.

Nevertheless, "ridership" in the church continues to diminish. Despite the best strategic planning, fewer and fewer people come to church. Denominations close churches, amalgamate congregations, and downsize staff.

Finally, the day comes when pastors are greeted at the front door by a different kind of visitor: a seeker. Before the pastor can ask, "Where to, lady?" the seeker says, "Where are *you* going, Reverend?"

He smiles warmly. "Why, we'll give you a ride around the Christian year!"

The seeker looks puzzled. "What for, Reverend?"

The pastor hands her some coffee. "Why, you can show your children the old faith neighborhood where you grew up, and you can honor the memory of your dear old mum."

The woman looks at the pastor a long time. Finally she says, "No thanks, Reverend," and walks away.

The bottom line in the twenty-first century is that fewer and fewer people want to just ride around the Christian year just to return to the front doors of the church.

## The Meandering Dilettante

Sociologists have long observed that religious institutions tend to preserve heritage ties, cultural homogeneity, and family bonds. They protect a common language, entrench traditional behavior patterns, and elevate tribal symbols of unity. Since they are scientists concerned with measurable facts, sociologists tend to avoid questions about the truth that lies behind all of these things. They translate the goal of discipleship to mean acculturation or membership assimilation.

The habit of thinking once associated with scientific sociology has now become the habit of thinking of church leaders and veteran church members. It is a supposed objectivity that has come to dominate North American educational systems and society as a whole. Huston Smith describes this "scientism" in his recent book *Why Religion Matters: The Fate of the Human Spirit in an Age of Disbelief* (San Francisco: HarperSanFrancisco, 2001). He argues that what was once a small philosophical movement has become a pervasive modern worldview, in which truth and reality are arbitrarily limited to what is self-evident, measurable, quantifiable, and therefore practical. Smith challenges the presumption of this worldview, and warns of dire consequences to the human spirit when the significance of nonquantifiable truths are ignored or shrugged off onto esoteric professional priests.

Here is the dire consequence for the church. What was once a blessed side effect of faith community has become the primary goal of faith community. The goal of the church is not discipleship, but acculturation. The purpose of the religious institution is not to reach out, but to draw in. The mission of the organization is not to risk all for immeasurable outcomes of abundant life in relationship to God, but to risk a percentage of income and three blocks of time per week in order to preserve heritage, a rather tame universal friendliness, and an all too Western and simplistic view of family life.

The long-term effect of this worldview is that churches tend to welcome and encourage spiritual dilettantes who meander their way through daily life, and turn away and discourage passionate seekers who want to go deep and are prepared to radically alter daily lifestyle. The latter are "fanatics," and the former are "our kind of people." Dilettantes are curious about religion and passionate about institutional budgets. They want their children to attend Sunday school to be acculturated to become good citizens, good family members, or good students, but they themselves will only attend Sunday worship and occasional meetings. The liberal version of the spiritual dilettante hesitates to use the name "Jesus" for fear that somebody will take offense, the truth behind the name being of less concern than awkward breaches in neighborliness or the pragmatic impact on charitable contributions. The conservative version of spiritual dilettante always uses the name "Jesus" as a dogmatic shield to protect them from serious conversation with seekers outside the arena of cultural accommodation.

As I trace the spiritual journey of the "meandering dilettante," note the hidden worldview of scientism. What matters is the reasonableness of faith and the explanation of facts. (See figure 3A.)

Like a good sociologist of religion, the church assumes that the public is fundamentally neutral in its opinion of the church. Members of the public observe church people behaving in odd ways, but do not understand it. Therefore, the church informs the visiting public's intellectual database. This is the educational methodology of pragmatism. Teach people to read, and their lives will improve. Print warnings on every package of cigarettes, and people will stop smoking. Explain the odd behavior of church people, and the reasonable benefits of belonging to the institution

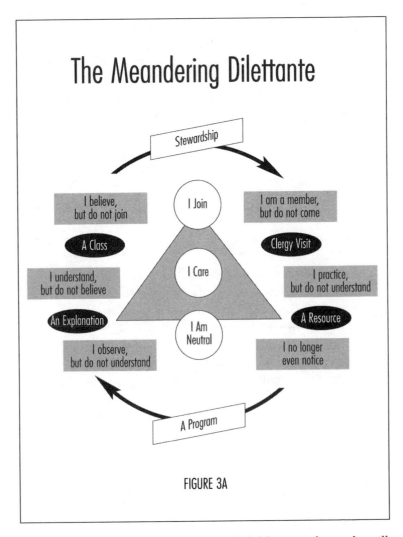

# The Meandering Dilettante

FIGURE 3A

for the sake of roots, friendship, and children, and people will come.

Once they understand church practice, offer them a classroom (seminar, continuing education forum, or expository preaching) so that eventually they can understand the faith. Make the faith as reasonable and rational as possible. Describe faith as an insurance policy for eternal salvation, or as a blueprint for social change.

Eventually, individuals will publicly declare that they are sane, reasonable people who have studied the right books, understood the correct information, and are prepared to declare allegiance to the denominational franchise. They join. Joining the church offers them various membership privileges (free weddings, constant attention from clergy, comfortable assurance, and practical coaching through all the life cycles). In return, they participate in the stewardship program, offering negotiable percentages of their money, time, and talent for the institutional agenda.

If some experience of unexplainable evil or some internal, hurtful conflict intrudes on the person's life, the meandering dilettante will drop out of the institution. She or he will cease worship attendance, but adamantly remain a voting member. This individual may even attend other support groups, and participate in other service clubs, but will retain control of the church. Spirituality may be mysterious, and can safely be left to professional clergy, but the meandering dilettante remains involved in what is really important, namely, institutional policy that influences heritage, fellowship, and family.

Unless the clergy visit the person to explain gratuitous evil or resolve conflict, the meandering dilettante will step farther away from the church. He or she will practice personal faith, but will not understand why. These individuals eat fish on Fridays, but don't know why. They are compelled to give up things in February and March, but don't know why. They attend Christmas Eve services, but don't understand what is happening. Unless a video or print resource is given to them—or better yet, an official directive from the denominational head office—they will drop out altogether and no longer notice the church. The only way to restart their involvement is to persuade them to take a new course of study or become involved in a crisis intervention program.

Note especially that meandering dilettantes tend to match their involvement with the church with their personal life cycles. They become more active when children and grandchildren are involved, and less active if they are single adults or empty-nesters. They become passionate about membership privileges around baptisms, weddings, and funerals, and indifferent to membership obligations in times of financial growth and good health. The meandering dilettante eventually wanders away from the church, but only after effectively blocking the influx of passionate seekers. (See figure 3B.)

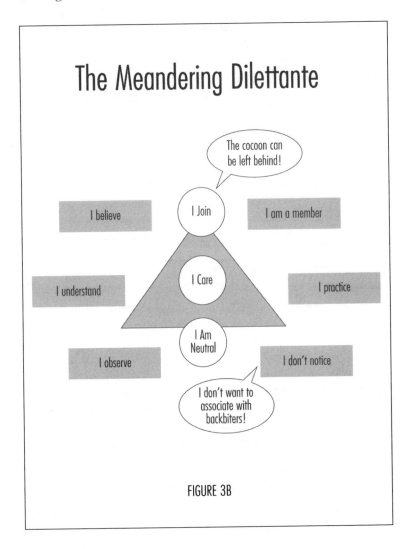

FIGURE 3B

Meandering dilettantes readily wander away from church membership. On the one hand, at the peak of their involvement they discover they no longer *need* the church. The need for roots, friendliness, and support for child rearing is being met in other ways. Religion is an esoteric mystery, but religions are basically the same, so they will dabble in various faiths and philosophies as whim or circumstance require. The church is all right, but they don't *need* it anymore. On the other hand, the more they react to conflict or pain, the more they discover they do not *want* the church. The church failed in its promise. It could not explain gratuitous evil. The clergy were too busy to visit. The resources failed to protect them from cultural diversity, failed to ensure the survival of their marriages, and failed to keep their kids from drugs. The church is a scam, and they are outraged by betrayal.

As the worldview of scientism expands, and as the church fails to deliver on its traditional sociological promise to protect heritage, build harmony, and preserve family, meandering dilettantes are running faster and faster out of the church.

## The Lost Crusaders

The first Crusade launched by the passionate preaching of Bernard of Clairveaux produced unexpected results. On the one hand, it contributed to the demise of medieval feudalism, encouraged the growth of the middle class, and actually led to the restoration of self-esteem and political rights for the poor. On the other hand, it did *not* lead to the enduring recovering of Jerusalem, peace for the Middle East, or justice for the persecuted (Christian, Muslim, or Jew). The actual experience of the first crusaders was one of modest victory and eventual discouragement. They did temporarily recover the Holy Land, but according to the testimony of many of the knights, they "got lost" along the way. They got lost geographically and spiritually. Many diverted their militant energies away from the recovery of the Holy Land to sack Constantinople or establish their own kingdoms in Sicily and Odessa. Many more simply returned home disappointed.

As an alternative to the meanderings of spiritual dilettantes, many Christian individuals and churches have gone crusading. The causes vary. Some are left-wing causes concerned with gender equality, reproductive choice, capitalist oppression, and sexual orientation. Some are right-wing causes concerned with family values, the pro-life movement, hard work, and sexual reorientation. The particular cause is not really relevant to the ability of the church to thrive. Launched by the passionate preaching of Martin Luther King Jr., for example, the Civil Rights movement enlisted many leaders eager to recover Jerusalem, and to bring peace to America and justice to the oppressed. The good that was accomplished was often unexpected. The goals sought after were only temporarily achieved. The experience of many of these "Knights Templar" was that somewhere they got lost—geographically and spiritually—along the way.

Huston Smith argues in *Why Religion Matters* that in addition to the scientism that has colored the worldview of North Americans, traditional sources of social reform have also limited and distorted the authentic spirituality of the earliest church.

- Higher education has shifted public sensibilities from belief, to nonbelief, to disbelief, bracketing religious experience into ever-narrower compartments of emotionalism, psychology, or acculturation. Smith quotes Asian art historian A. K. Coomaraswamy, educated in North America, as saying that "several decades as an immigrant had convinced him that it takes four years to acquire a college education in America and forty [years] to get over it" (p. 102).
- The media has generally treated religion as a peculiar activity that rational people generally avoid. Churches are made to look like cults. Religion, at best, is made to look like a social service, and at worst is made to look like mild insanity. Smith quotes Peter Jennings warning: "We must stop treating religion as if it were like building model airplanes, just another hobby, not really a fit activity for intelligent adults" (p. 120).

- The law has managed to marginalize religion through the very process of legitimizing its right of expression. The public can afford to be open-minded about religion in schools or the charitable status of religious institutions because ultimately it doesn't matter too much. Its most practical value is as a marketing vehicle to package particular political points of view. Smith quotes Boris Yeltsin responding to an American reporter's question about his religious beliefs. "No, I am not religious," Yeltsin said, "but I *am* superstitious" (p. 122).

These developments have had dire consequences on the future of vital churches. The more ideologically driven the crusaders became, the more the church agenda began to be shaped by the battle to control higher education, the media, and the law. The real victory, however, was won neither by the left nor the right, but by higher education, the media, and the law, which managed to co-opt Christian mission with their own hidden assumptions.

- Clergy graduates from seminary are ill equipped to converse with culture, resorting to dogmatic pronouncements or psychological rationalizations, and are totally confused about how to interact with the seeking public. The few that do not burn out or change career paths, and manage to grow a church, frequently comment that it took three years to acquire a seminary degree and ten years to get over it.
- Churches have generally adopted marketing strategies that reflect their low self-esteem and anxiety about media condemnation. The good news is not one of radical forgiveness, inclusiveness, and apocalyptic blessing, but rather that the church isn't really as bad as you might think.
- Denominations have increasingly placed their fate in the hands of lawyers who know better than volunteers the intricacies of litigation against personnel and

property, but who are not particularly sympathetic with the core values, beliefs, or mission of their clients. If anything, the social agenda of left- and right-wing churches is shaped primarily by smart lawyers, constant political lobbies, and good luck.

The fundamental problem faced by the crusaders of the twenty-first century is that they can no longer tell the difference between a church and a nonprofit agency. Not only have the battles waged in education, media, and law required a strategic shift from mission by congregation to mission by agency, but also the outcome of these battles has been that agencies tend to be more credible to the IRS and more effective amid corporate industry. The crusaders feel unity, do good work, talk about spirituality, but rarely attend worship, personally visit strangers in the hospital, or read their Bibles daily. Although active in a nonprofit corporation, they occasionally feel an ache for something mission-related, and put it down to lingering superstition.

As I trace the spiritual journey of the lost crusaders, note the hidden confusion between nonprofit status and faith community. What is important is winning control of educational institutions, media, and the law. The "spiritual stuff" we can all talk about later in the pub or potluck supper. (See figure 3C.)

Like a zealous nonprofit organization, the church assumes that the general public is blind to its cause. Such is the blurring between the boundaries of church and agency that regardless of whether the cause of blindness is sin or society, the result is much the same. People admire their reformer's cause or commitment, but do not understand it, so the church raises their consciousness through symbolic deeds and social critique. Once people identify with the cause, they are trained for articulate advocacy and social service. They "take up the cross," and are assigned a position in the ranks according to their talent. Their cause resembles the quest for the Holy Grail.

If others do not listen to the logic of the cause, or reject it outright, church members become resigned to failure. They are less active, but their outlook becomes more rigid and judgmental

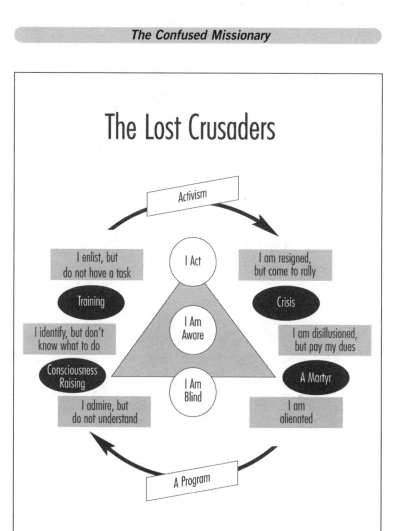

# The Lost Crusaders

Activism

I enlist, but do not have a task

I Act

I am resigned, but come to rally

Training

Crisis

I identify, but don't know what to do

I Am Aware

I am disillusioned, but pay my dues

Consciousness Raising

I Am Blind

A Martyr

I admire, but do not understand

I am alienated

A Program

FIGURE 3C

They are the "true believers" and the "righteous few," a self-con-
sciousness celebrated and entrenched in regular worship or large
rallies. Unless a particular crisis emerges to mobilize them again,
their increasing disillusionment will cause them to stop attending
worship or rallies, even though they will continue to pay their
pledge (dues) to the institution. Eventually only a martyr will
energize their renewed interest. If the leaders they most admired

are imprisoned or persecuted, their indignation will again rise up and motivate them to participate in a new program for the cause.

The reality is that the more preoccupied the church becomes with control of education, media, and law, the more hidden assumptions within these disciplines limit or distort the deeper and more holistic experience of the spirit. (See figure 3D.)

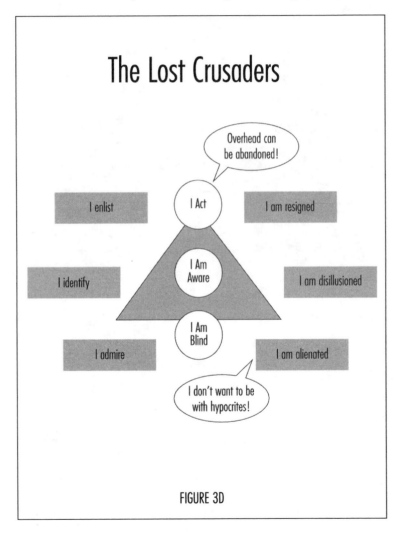

FIGURE 3D

Lost crusaders also readily depart from church membership. At the peak of their involvement, the confusion between church and agency is complete. Crusaders weary of what they consider unnecessary baggage of property, liturgy, or personnel. They become frustrated that money is wasted on ideologically incorrect curricula, or that time is wasted on mere fellowship and institutional maintenance. The overhead can be abandoned. On the other hand, from the depths of their alienation they become convinced that the church was never really serious about the cause in the first place. They don't want to have anything to do with the church.

As the confusion between church and nonprofit agency accelerates, more and more people reject the church as inefficient. Nominations and offices become a waste of time. Obsession with property and heritage undermines credibility for the cause in the eyes of the public, and threaten the charitable tax status the agency requires. The lost crusaders decide the recovery of Jerusalem was a tactical mistake to begin with, and sack Constantinople or conquer Sicily instead.

## *Interpreting the Facts*

Obtaining data about congregational life and mission is a notoriously difficult thing to do. Over three hundred thousand Christian congregations exist in the United States alone, and many faith communities are not aligned with a denomination. Some may have no fixed address, professional clergy to contact, or consistent leaders with whom to communicate. The most significant information that reveals the true state of life and mission is often difficult to quantify. Since the major metaphor for the church is organic, rather than institutional, a comparison can be made with the interpretive task of physicians. Scientific medical research can gather measurable data about the efficiency and durability of the human body, but the personal physician has a long-term relationship with a patient and can better interpret the quality of his or her life and holistic health. In the same way, sociologists of religion can gather measurable data about congregational organization and program, but it requires the combined objective *and* intuitive insight of a physician who is intimately connected with the patient to interpret the organization's real vitality and well-being. The whole is more than the sum of statistics.

Many small and large sociological studies have been done in recent years. The fact that foundations and denominations have significantly increased funding for such research indicates the growing consternation that something is wrong with the patient. For my purposes, I limit my reference here to four studies: *The Multiracial Congregations Project* (Michael Emerson, Rice University), the *Organizing Religious Work Project* (Nancy Ammerman, Hartford Institute for Religion Research), *The National Congregations Study* (Mark Chaves, University of Arizona), and the most extensive study of all, *Faith Communities Today* (F.A.C.T.) (Carl Dudley and David Roozen, Hartford Institute for Religion Research). The most optimistic report is the recent F.A.C.T. research, and that will be the primary focus of these comments. As a "physician" raising alarm about the overall "health" of the body of Christ, it seems appropriate to critique the most optimistic of reports from the "medical researchers."

As a necessary preface to my comments, I need to reflect on both the methodology of sociological research about congregational life and mission, as well as the manner in which such research is received. This is a relevant digression, because it helps explain why all of these sociological studies have generally failed to help the confused missionary become any less confused. Many clergy and lay church leaders read these reports with high expectation, and are disappointed. Occasionally, sociologists of religion have offered remedies to cure or refresh the body of Christ, but to the perception of ministry practitioners the remedies seem impractical or repetitious of old programs that didn't work.

The reason for this seeming disconnection between the value of sociological research and the efficacy of church renewal has to do with the methodological assumptions of the scientific researchers.

1. *Sociologists only ask questions of church* insiders. The *Faith Communities Today* researchers, for example, sent the questionnaires to the core leaders or regular participants of churches, most of which are declining in participation and struggling to gain leadership. Many of the questions asked these insiders for their opinions about whether the church was effective in mission, welcoming to the community, and so forth. *The National Congregations Study* sought to obtain a random sampling of religious organizations by simply asking a random sampling of individuals about the religious organization to which they belonged. The researchers then backtracked to the organization, and then relied on the clergy, a staff person, or core lay leader as their key informant. Serious research among dropouts, marginalized Christians, and the institutionally alienated and seeking public is usually ignored, or is rarely used to critique the opinions that church insiders have of themselves. No matter how astute these clergy and core leaders might be, they are on the inside looking out, and are still largely content with the status quo. Of course people on the inside think their congregation is friendly. Of course clergy and staff members think their congregation is effective in mission.

   In all fairness to the researchers, the funding they receive from denominations and foundations limits them severely. The information they gather from marginal, alienated, or seeking people is piecemeal, and rarely used as a reality check for the surveys taken from church insiders. (Researcher Kirk Hadaway shared remarkable videotaped interviews with such people, but to my knowledge the information, so revealing of the shortcomings of modern churches, has yet to be shared beyond the discussions of a few denominational leaders.) Researchers from *The Multiracial Congregations Project* were able to deploy four people, for two weeks, in four metropolitan areas.

The sampling may be an accurate reflection of the country, but how profound can the final diagnosis and prescription be when in such a short time their interviews are limited to clergy, church members, and others recommended by the clergy and the church members?

2. *Sociologists keep looking for universal trends in an era when contextuality is everything.* Their generalizations are fewer and fewer, and mean less and less. Consider these few selected findings from *The National Congregations Study:*

- most of the resources are in the fewest churches;
- worship and education are the core activities of religious organizations;
- the public sectors in which congregations are most involved are education and arts;
- participation is not necessarily drawn from the immediate neighborhood;
- recently founded congregations have more contemporary worship and less mission outreach than do older established churches.

Interesting as that might be, of what practical benefit is this information for church leaders seeking to expand mission or reverse decline in their particular local context?

The Hartford Institute offers an interactive page on its Web site (FACT@hartsem.edu), with which church leaders can compare various aspects of their church organization and program to other congregations in their denomination or other denominations. Fifteen questions are asked, and the comparison is limited by eleven measurable fields (region, race, finance, location, adult participation, music, year of founding, five-year membership trends, self-perceived spiritual vitality, denomination, and the occurrence of recent conflict). Yet what does this comparison actually accomplish? On the one hand, it encourages a kind of resigned fatalism on the part of many churches, because they see that their situation (within these limited fields) is normative everywhere else, and if nobody else can change, they won't either. On the other hand, it may reveal that a congregation is abnormal, and that in order to be healthy it needs to match the normative pattern and get in step with all the rest of the declining churches in the country.

In all fairness to the researchers, their real goal is not to help congregations thrive in their unique contexts, but to help them discern their place in the normative experience of churches across the country. Among church participants and the seeking public, however, the distinction is missed. The boundary between what is normative, common, and general, and what is faithful, unique, and missional, is blurred. Church leaders use the research to help the church become "normal," or to accept being "normal," when in fact the local church is called to be faithful. Growing and vital churches are the anomalies in the pattern of Christendom.

3. *Sociologists are limited by the very objectivity they value.* As scientists, they rely only on measurable data that can be quantified, and eventually developed into a bar graph. Therefore, they focus on things like structure, program, personnel, and money. The trouble is that these objectivities are the very things that are *least relevant* to the vitality of congregational life and mission. The real dilemma of the church is that the structure is sound, the program is clear, the personnel are available, and the money is out there—and the church is declining. The issues that are *most relevant* to thriving congregational life and mission are not quantifiable. They are qualitative. These issues include the spiritual transformations of people, daily lifestyle of members, the spontaneous and daring deeds of leaders, the

human energy and concentration devoted to mission, and the "heart" of the body of Christ. The more contextual, fast-paced, and culturally interconnected the world becomes, the more such qualitative issues are decisive for the future of the church.

As valuable as sociological research might be to cultural observers, for those eager to be faithful in following Jesus into the mission field, the findings of much of the research seems like swatting flies and swallowing camels. When sociologists do seek to measure the really significant, contextual, qualitative issues, their preoccupation with objectivity gets in the way. What they measure is not the friendliness of a congregation, but the opinions of church insiders about friendliness. What they measure is not the relevance and effectiveness of mission for personal and social change, but the number of Scouting programs and food banks funded by the church budget or housed in the church building.

In all fairness to the researchers, they can't really do anything else. They would likely say, "If we didn't quantify and generalize, we wouldn't be researchers and scientists." Yet that is precisely the point. Church vitality isn't really a scientific investigative field at all. It is intuitive, contextual, holistic, and qualitative. The keys to faithful mission and church vitality are not likely to be revealed by scientific research, just as the keys to quality of life and personal fulfillment are not likely to be revealed by medical researchers. The human life, like the body of Christ, has a mystery and significance that is beyond the ken of science.

Now it is clearer why this digression about the methodology of sociological research is relevant to my description of the "confused missionary." The best and most expert sociologists would actually accept the limitations of their work articulated here. The problem is that church leaders, members, and the general public do not. Decades ago scientists made exaggerated claims about the universal applicability of their discernment of truth, and the general public was skeptical. Today the best scientists are very reserved about the universal significance of their discernment of truth, and it is the general public who exaggerates it. This is the "scientism" against which Huston Smith warns in his book *Why Religion Matters*. This is how that modern cultural bias is revealed in the very hearts of church leaders and church members.

With these methodological reservations, let us look carefully at the research from that most optimistic of studies, *Faith Communities Today*. I focus on each of the six major topics of the report, and connect them to the paradigms of meandering dilettante and the lost crusaders.

## Basic Demographics

The basic demographics of the church beg the questions "Is the glass half empty or half full?" and "Is the glass getting emptier or fuller?"

- Half the congregations in the United States have fewer than one hundred regularly participating adults.
- Slightly more than half the congregations are in town or rural settings.
- More than half of the congregations were organized before 1945.

If those small congregations were new start churches, the situation would be more promising. However, those small churches are not new. Most were organized before 1945, or in the post-war boom of the 1950s. They are located in rural areas from which the population is migrating, and are usually *not* located in the urban centers to which people are going. Small congregations are usually older and predominantly female, and young people are less likely to join them because often the older people refuse to adapt and the small churches don't have many resources.

Meandering dilettantes will keep these small churches open for as long as they can through memorials, bequests, and emergency fund-raising. The historic location, the quaint facility, and the old-fashioned technology will be too precious to them to change. However, these meandering dilettantes will eventually meander to Florida or die. Meanwhile, the lost crusaders will increasingly resent the amount of money required to maintain these small churches, and the deployment of personnel wasted among declining populations. They will increase pressure to raise capital for their cause through the sale of useless properties. In short, about 50 percent of the congregations in the United States are in serious jeopardy of amalgamation and closure in the next twenty years. Meandering dilettantes will buy them for personal cottages, and lost crusaders will convert them to community centers.

The F.A.C.T. study found that most worshipers did not travel very far to get to church (less than the distance to work), but I am more inclined to believe *The National Congregations Study*, which discovered that congregations are not necessarily oriented to the community or neighborhood in which they are located. A significant proportion of worshipers travel as much as thirty minutes to church. Meandering dilettantes will bypass any number of churches to reach the residence of their sentimentality, and lost crusaders are apt to travel far to be among those who share the ideological or dogmatic cause. The increasing indifference of churches (especially suburban churches) to the experienced needs of the local neighborhood and community accelerates the indifference of the community to them.

The F.A.C.T. study found that most congregations are white (76 percent). This statistic on race should raise eyebrows about the accuracy of the survey, since African American, Asian American, and Hispanic American churches are among the fastest growing and rapidly multiplying faith communities in the country. However, they are often not aligned, structured, wealthy, or professionally staffed, and therefore an objective survey has trouble measuring their existence. Indeed, the F.A.C.T. study reveals that Sunday morning is no more sensitive to racial and cultural diversity than worship at any other time. This suggests that race and culture, not mission or spiritual growth, is the real glue that holds many congregations together. As the public becomes increasingly cross-cultural, these churches stick out as anachronistic anomalies nobody finds credible, despite the fact that more than half of the congregations founded after 1966 think of themselves as "open to innovation." Both meandering dilettantes and lost crusaders are remarkably indifferent to racism as a matter of personal lifestyle.

Congregations are predominantly female (66 percent), and oriented to families with kids at home and to seniors aged sixty and older. This may be good news to some crusaders with a feminist agenda, and to some dilettantes fueling the myth that the youth are the future of the church, but generally this has proved to be a recipe for decline. Males have fewer role models for Christian lifestyle and leadership, and the children grow up, go to college, and relocate. The meandering dilettantes are usually overzealous in the church while the kids are at home, and remarkably sporadic in involvement afterward. The biggest danger in this pattern is that the minority of children who grow up in such an environment later move to the suburbs and plant a new church on similar lines. The greater resources of the suburb sustain the strategy of ministry among families with kids at home and seniors aged sixty and older who find kids cute for a time; but the cult of harmony soon plateaus church growth.

## Sources of Unity and Cohesion

The organization of the *Faith Communities Today* study seems to suggest that the sources of unity in the church are denominational loyalty, clarity of purpose, and high moral standards. But as I have already pointed out, the *real* source of cohesion is racial and cultural uniformity. This is true for both meandering dilettantes and lost crusaders. Both actually tend to distance themselves from controversial or "incorrect" denominational policy, have little purpose beyond survival or the achievement of a limited political or dogmatic end, and experience remarkable scandal regarding the behavior of their members and personnel.

The F.A.C.T. study reports that 62 percent of congregations *say* that they reflect clear expressions of the denominational heritage. That, of course, is the problem. Can you trust their self-perceptions? Most denominational leaders do not. They know that the perceptions of denominational ethos vary enormously from context to context, and that in the end it is the local mythology that wins out over denominational policy every time. The more cross-cultural the community becomes, the less relevant denominational heritage becomes.

Perhaps what is more revealing is that even in this most optimistic of reports, 38 percent of the congregations say they do not express denominational heritage well. (This 38 percent is a combined total of three categories in which participants were asked how well they express denominational heritage. Of those, 25 percent answered "somewhat"; 10 percent answered "slightly"; and 3 percent answered that they do this "not at all"!) They don't really care about it! This bodes ill for any denomination seeking to appoint clergy from the judicatory head office. Oddly enough, this statistic does not seem to alarm the researchers very much. Yet one wonders what the head office of Holiday Inn would think if a study revealed that 38 percent of their franchises did not express the corporate identity of Holiday Inn very well. I suspect that would be a source of considerable anxiety. Even so, the future viability of denominations is in serious jeopardy. That is not a small risk to the local congregation, because most congregations (especially that 50 percent with fewer than one hundred adults in attendance) rely on the capital pools, personnel deployment, and program resources generated by those greatly weakened denominations. The F.A.C.T. study reveals that over 56 percent of the congregations "high on denominational heritage" are experiencing serious difficulty with their financial health.

The methodological preoccupation with objectivity is particularly misleading when the source of unity and cohesion is linked to religious authority. Once again, these statistics are based on what congregations say about themselves. According to the study,

Baptists are oriented to Scripture, Lutherans and Episcopalians are oriented to creeds and traditions, Assemblies of God and Nazarenes are oriented to the authority of Spirit, and Unitarians are oriented to human reason. Everybody else is somewhere in between. That these are the *real* sources of unity and cohesion, however, will come as a surprise to most of the pastors in these churches. What people say and how they behave in daily life or even congregational life are very different things. Meandering dilettantes are very pragmatic about their appeals to authority, and generally live by their own biases during the week. Lost crusaders are very restrictive about their appeals to authority, and generally live by their own interpretations of these supposed authorities. The one thing they share is a passion for control, and not their readiness to surrender to authority.

The F.A.C.T. study reports that 85 percent of the congregations in the United States believe that they have high clarity of vitality and vision. Frankly, this will come as a shock to most church leaders in both congregation and judicatory, because the general consensus is that vitality and vision are precisely what 85 percent of the churches do not have. According to the report, over 58 percent of United States congregations in every demographic context consider themselves to be vitally alive, and over 50 percent of all congregations consider themselves to be moral beacons. Frankly, this will come as a shock to marginal members, church dropouts, and most of the general public. According to the report, well over 50 percent of churches in every demographic context feel "high excitement about the future," and over 50 percent of these churches believe they enjoy a "high involvement of teens." This will come as a shock to all pastors struggling to upgrade their worship technologies, and to high school teachers and youth workers in general.

The lack of any "reality testing" among congregations surveyed is astonishing. If the study reveals anything, it is the remarkable naïveté among the core church participants surveyed. And yet that is the hallmark of both meandering dilettantes and lost crusaders. Both groups are simply out of touch with the reality of their context and the real effectiveness of their ministry.

Dilettantes are caught up in sentimentality and homogenous cultural values that they project on others. Crusaders are caught up in an ideological or dogmatic agenda that they impose on others. Neither group really listens to the public.

The logic of the F.A.C.T. researchers is correct. Churches with clarity of purpose should be vital and visionary, moral beacons to the community, excited and open to the future, and particularly attractive to youth. In fact, however, most churches in North America are none of those things. They are declining in membership, attendance, credibility, and impact. The fact that the core members and leaders of these churches do not recognize this is the greatest worry of all. If indeed they are not experienced by the public as vital, visionary, moral, open, or attractive to youth, then they must not have clarity of purpose.

The F.A.C.T. study notes that there is a correlation between clarity of purpose and high membership expectations, and that as congregations age both clarity and rigor decline. Once this data is tested against the actual behavior of congregations, this generalization will change. The real correlation is between cultural homogeneity and high membership expectations. Churches may live in a fog about purpose, but they expect members to accept and celebrate homogenous cultural forms, attitudes, and behavior patterns. This has nothing to do with scripture, creeds, human reason, or the Holy Spirit. It has everything to do with music, local heritage, matriarchal and patriarchal bias, and ideological agenda.

## Growth, Change, and Conflict

The real sources of coherence and unity are actually identified in this section. However, while the F.A.C.T. study finally identifies the real reasons modern churches stay together, the study is less accurate in revealing exactly how much these factors truly promote growth. After all, while their research suggests that 50 percent of all congregations are growing, it also implies that 50 percent of all congregations are *not* growing. I rank the sources of coherence and growth in order of importance:

1. *Cultural affinity, finding "our kind of people."* Congregations actually discourage cultural diversity in favor of enlisting microcultures that model the lifestyles, attitudes, and perspectives of core controllers. However, as microcultures in North America multiply, each subculture has fewer participants, and it becomes harder and harder to grow a congregation to more than three hundred members.

2. *Community involvement, keeping in touch.* Congregations are only partly concerned about outreach for its own purpose. Instead, outreach (including everything from Boy Scouts to food banks) is really a sophisticated method of identifying and recruiting "our kind of people" who will turn around and support the church institution.

3. *Personal support and discipline of church insiders.* Congregations offer excellent membership privileges to newcomers, and hold their staff and board accountable for members' protection.

4. *Inspirational and uplifting worship.* Among meandering dilettantes, this implies worship done well in limited aesthetic genres. Among lost crusaders, this implies politically correct liturgy and dogmatically pure symbols.

5. *Focused organizational programming.* Congregations implement well-organized and sufficiently resourced programs for education and outreach. Dilettantes prefer children's ministries; crusaders prefer adult advocacy; both focus on youth ministries.

6. *Promotional marketing.* The F.A.C.T. study confirms that this really is not intended to produce growth, but it is not about strengthening congregational vitality either. It has most to do with sustaining a congregational self-image or mythos that is rarely tested with the public.

The F.A.C.T. study is certainly correct that outreach, program focus, healthy relationships, high membership expectations, and uplifting contemporary worship all promote church growth, but the question is "Are churches *really* doing these things?" The study asks core church participants to offer an opinion about whether or not they are growing, but it is unclear whether or not they are using these same criteria.

Both meandering dilettantes and lost crusaders tend to use "growth" as an industrial metaphor. They measure growth in objective ways appreciated by sociologists. Is membership increasing? Is the budget increasing? Are programs multiplying? Is the property being improved? Is everybody happy? They do not tend to use "growth" as an organic metaphor, and key (less scientific) questions are rarely answered. Are adults really going deeper in their relationship with God? Are more microcultures finding ways to hook into congregational life? Are lay ministries expanding? Are lifestyles being changed to the image of Christ? Is the world and our neighborhood really any different this month because we existed?

This partly explains the preoccupation of churches and the F.A.C.T. research with family-based ministries. It is not surprising that the research reveals that family-based congregations sustain membership growth. It is surprising that researchers and congregational leaders do not recognize the fragility that implies for the faith community. As traditional, Western family structures break down, so also do traditional churches become less attractive to the public. It may be that 72 percent of growing churches succeed by emphasizing family-based ministries, but will that strategy continue to work? After all, in the 1950s probably 95 percent of growing churches attributed success to family-based ministries.

As I read through the data on growth, change, and conflict, certain lessons become clear that should be alarming to church leaders for the future.

- *The smaller the church is, the less open it is to change.* Since 50 percent of congregations involve fewer than one hundred adults, this should make leaders squirm. The very churches that are closest to closure, and which probably need to make radical changes more than anyone else, are the very churches that resist it most. F.A.C.T. researchers concluded from the self-perceptions of leaders that older congregations are more likely to change worship, while newer congregations think they are already contemporary and need not change. This is inaccurate, because no one has discerned what kinds of changes these churches are really willing to make. What the research really reveals is that older churches are more ready to make minimal changes to worship, and that newer congregations are less willing to make minimal changes to worship.

• *Younger congregations are generally more (not less) deluded than older congregations.* This sounds harsh, but younger meandering dilettantes tend to have more resources to bolster their illusions than do older ones, and younger lost crusaders tend to have preserved their idealism more than have older ones. This is suggested in the F.A.C.T. research itself. The research suggest that 56 percent of congregations founded between 1966 and 1989 (67 percent of congregations founded after 1990) claim to be open to innovation. However, when it comes to supposedly "contemporary" worship, only 27 percent (33 percent) of these same "young" congregations regularly use electronic keyboards. Only 24 percent (27 percent) regularly use electric bass guitar. Only 25 percent (30 percent) regularly use drums or other percussion. The general public has to ask: "That's innovative?"

• *Moderate and liberal churches are* less open *to change than anybody else.* Despite all the boasting about inclusiveness, prophetic witness, and contemporaneity, moderate and liberal churches score lower than other groups (including evangelicals, African American, Catholic, and Orthodox) on enthusiasm in welcoming new members. Of course, everybody scores rather badly on this, with non-Christian groups (especially

Muslim and Baha'is) scoring as being most enthusias-
tic. If there is a "treasure" contained in the earthen ves-
sels of either dilettante or crusading churches, they
seem remarkably loathe to share it.

Finally, it is no surprise that conflict grows worse as worship
changes or financial debts increase. However, the F.A.C.T.
research reveals that it is not as bad as meandering dilettantes or
lost crusaders imagine. These churches tend to exaggerate the
worry, obsessed that even the smallest change will fracture the
cult of harmony and exclude a veteran member. To be sure, 59
percent of congregations experiencing significant worship change
also experience serious conflict, and 73 percent experience serious conflict in the midst of severe financial challenge. On the
other hand, 41 percent and 27 percent respectively do *not* experience serious conflict. People are always more ready to change
than either the dilettante or the crusader are willing to admit.

## Congregational Life

The *Faith Communities Today* study seems to state the obvious
by concluding that worship and religious education (primarily
Sunday school for children) are the core activities of most
churches, and that this leads most churches to intersect with public life primarily in matters of education and fine arts. This under-
scores the fact that the coherence and unity of most churches lies
in a homogeneous culture that has little to do with either mission
or theology. Aesthetics, not doctrine, is now at the heart of most
North American churches, which explains why music, not theology, is at the root of most controversies. Traditional educational
methodology aimed at the assimilation of children or youth into
the organizational culture, rather than creative communications
aimed at equipping members for outreach, lies at the heart of
most congregations. This explains why control of curricula and
liturgies ("proper education" and "good worship") is also at the
root of most controversies.

Although the F.A.C.T. study still tends to survey the opinions of insiders, rather than the nuances of congregational behavior, the research is still revealing and alarming.

1. *Worship and spirituality.* The vast majority of congregations emphasize preaching and worship on the themes of "God's love and care" and "practical advice for daily living." Most of this is dependent on professionals, and over 80 percent of the churches rely on organ or classical piano support. In short, the laity are distanced from direct spiritual leadership and prefer it so. The clergy distance laity from direct spiritual leadership and prefer it so. The good news is that clergy coach laity with practical advice for daily living. The bad news is that laity cannot seem to coach themselves, and given the rise in litigation against clergy, the laity have less confidence that the clergy know what they are talking about. Meanwhile reassurances of God's love and care are supported by nonindigenous musical backgrounds, simultaneously reinforcing the cult of harmony and insulating the organization from outside intrusions.

   The F.A.C.T. researchers understand the importance of music as a marker to discern spiritual vitality. It is hard to understand, however, why they conclude that "larger congregations . . . use a broad array of alternatives to provide their members with a rich diet of music" (p. 41) based on the data they have uncovered.

- Even in the largest churches surveyed, no more than 3.7 instruments are frequently used in worship. Given that the organ and piano are two, what are the others? Perhaps an acoustic guitar, bells, or trumpets? We already know that fewer than 27 percent of young congregations use electric guitar.
- Interestingly, the F.A.C.T. research reveals that among those who regularly use electric guitar in worship, churches that emphasize scripture or Holy Spirit as pri-

mary sources of authority are by far more likely to do so (just below 100 percent of scripture-based churches and 80 percent of Holy Spirit-based churches, respectively). Meanwhile, fewer than 20 percent of those congregations that emphasize creeds, traditions, or human reason are likely to use an electric guitar. Although the distinctions between "evangelical" and "liberal" churches are breaking down, this still suggests that the churches most likely to decry culture use it, and the churches most likely to make claims of "relevance" do not.

• When it comes to spirituality, the F.A.C.T. study measures what congregations encourage their members to do, not what they actually do. Over 80 percent of congregations encourage members to do personal devotions, for example, but in the view of many church consultants, fewer than 5 percent of adults actually do them. This incredible discrepancy between intention and reality should alarm every church leader. Even in the earlier part of the twentieth century this discrepancy would not be so drastic. So what happened?

If anything, the F.A.C.T. study reveals how "untraditional" most modern traditional churches are. Their ancestors worshiped around themes of mission and discipleship, not pastoral care and privileges. Laity took initiative to be highly visible leaders in spiritual life. Although they used similar music and instruments, at the time they were indigenous to the population. The vast majority of adult participants took daily devotions and other spiritual disciplines very seriously.

2. *Congregational activities.* The paradox revealed in the F.A.C.T. study is that bigger churches with more resources have more programs, and the multiple programs generate more resources. This should come as alarming news to the 96 percent of the congregations

surveyed that have fewer than one thousand members. They are left out of the loop. If they are expecting denominational subsidies to assist them in getting into the loop, they had better think again. Denominations do not have the resources anymore.

The hidden paradox that is not addressed in the F.A.C.T. study is that while congregations indeed offer a vast array of programs for education, fellowship, service, performing arts, and sports, fewer and fewer people avail themselves of them. Sunday school enrollment is generally down, choirs scramble for members, youth groups come and go, and adult Bible studies languish. Consultants and denominational leaders observe that the smaller the church is, the larger the percentage of participation in its limited programs. The larger the church is, the smaller the percentage of participation in its many programs. Therefore, the hope of the small church is not resources, but involvement; and the peril of the large church is its overconfidence in resources and its lack of involvement.

3. *Community outreach.* The F.A.C.T. study confirms that vital congregations are involved in social services and justice advocacy, and the more outreach a church does the more vital it becomes. The priorities will vary from context to context. The unrealistic optimism emerges, however, when researchers assume that *what core leaders say they are doing is in fact what the church is doing, and when researchers assume that the extent and impact of these outreach programs are as significant as core leaders imagine.*

- The study concludes that more than two-thirds of all three hundred thousand congregations conservatively estimated to exist in North America support a thrift shop and more than one-third have tutoring programs for children. Yet this might mean simply that churches take a free-will offering for a thrift shop once a year, or that one or two former teachers who happen to be church members tutor kids in their spare time. The congregation doesn't "own" the ministry, doesn't pray regularly for the teachers, and may not even be aware of the program.

- Similarly, the study suggests that over 80 percent of congregations are involved in ministries offering food assistance, and 90 percent offer cash assistance. Consultants know, however, that in most churches this simply means that the professional clergy are authorized to use a small budget line to intervene whenever people in need stop by the office. Most likely there is no team of volunteers involved in the intervention, no systematic plan of lifestyle support, and the budget is severely limited.

It is not my purpose to be unduly pessimistic, or to depreciate these minor interventions, but to temper the unwarranted optimism of the report. While there is a connection between vitality and outreach, there is also a connection between the self-righteous delusions of church leaders and church decline.

More detail is offered in the *Organizing Religious Work Project*. From seven research sites, the study concludes that the average congregation provides money, volunteers, space, in-kind donations, and either staff or time or both to about six community outreach organizations. Two are usually direct services of food, clothing, or shelter; another two enhance education, health, and cultural life; the last two may be related to political advocacy, evangelism, or self-help. The more outreach a congregation does, the more vital it becomes; the more vital it becomes, the more outreach it does.

An average of six outreach programs in every congregation seems pretty good. The difficulty is that there is a continuum of involvement that dictates the degree to which such programs enhance congregational vitality. (See figure 3E.)

Most congregational support for outreach involves donations and property use. This actually leads to decreased church vitality

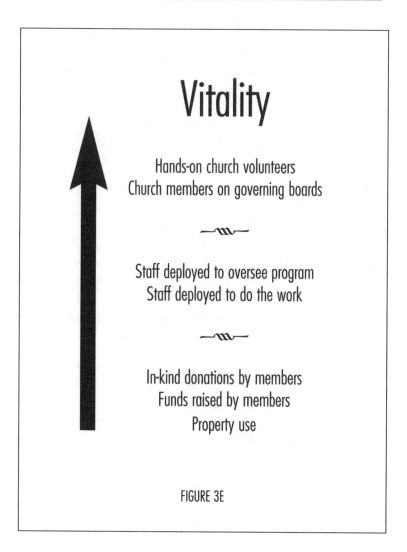

# Vitality

Hands-on church volunteers
Church members on governing boards

Staff deployed to oversee program
Staff deployed to do the work

In-kind donations by members
Funds raised by members
Property use

FIGURE 3E

Reliance on professional staff may or may not increase vitality. Church vitality only increases when church members are themselves intimately involved in the work or governance of the mission.

This, of course, is the way it used to be. Only in recent modern times have lazy churches opted to rent property and spend money as if that were genuine mission. Since the data doesn't reveal this, the best this study can do is ask leading questions at the end.

There is another alarming trend revealed in the studies about congregational vitality. In order to do effective outreach, congregations are increasingly dependent on partnership with other organizations. The *Organizing Religious Work* project finds that of the organizations with which congregations partner, 37 percent are religious nonprofits, 31 percent are secular nonprofits, 25 percent are informal networks, and 7 percent are government agencies. In the F.A.C.T. study, it appears that the more urbanized the context, the more interconnected congregational outreach will be with government agencies (at least in regard to day care or child care and health-related activities). This is understandable, in that the expense and complexity of mission have increased beyond the means of the average congregation.

What is alarming, however, is what happens to churches that do not have a clear sense of spiritual purpose or high expectation of discipleship for its members. The meandering dilettantes have no means of measuring compatibility between their core values and those of the external partner, and the lost crusaders have no desire to measure compatibility. The boundary between spiritual community and nonprofit agency becomes blurred, and the church is apt to take on the core values of the partner and shape its life around the partner's cause. Is this happening? Yes.

## Congregational Resources

The term "resource" is limited in the F.A.C.T. study to denominational materials (curricula, worship design materials, etc.), property, and money.

The research further alarms denominational leaders. The smaller the church is, the more likely it is to buy denominationally produced materials, but fewer than 50 percent of churches with 350 or more members are looking to denominational parents for their resources. This dooms denominational publishing houses, unless they expand their own markets, and compete for the attention of their own constituents. It signals the end to denominational loyalty. This might not be bad, except that one wonders to whom that loyalty will now be given? Meandering dilettantes are apt to give it to any organization that will enhance their cult of harmony (right or wrong), and lost crusaders are apt to give it to nonprofit agencies who single-mindedly support their cause. Torn between an obsession with "down home good feeling" and "political correctness," the general public is apt to look elsewhere for religious education and spiritual growth. Are they? Yes.

The F.A.C.T. study rightly identifies parking as a major issue. Almost half of all nonrural churches, and considerably more city-center churches, have acute parking problems. This reveals that their ancestors made an often-understandable tactical error in developing church property. What is alarming is that most churches ignore the significance of that tactical error, or refuse to do anything about it. The operative word here is "tactic." Tactics are not sacred, but changeable. The parking problem can be solved, even in the city center, if the congregation realizes its significance for growth and is prepared to change.

This issue is related to another F.A.C.T. discovery, namely, that the physical condition of church property is related to denominational pride. The more denominational pride (or pride in heritage), the more likely money and energy will be diverted to property maintenance. The operative word here is "pride." That same pride causes these churches to ignore the significance of property, and avoid making any serious changes that might involve demolition or construction, major landscaping, or relocation.

Most interesting is the discovery that problems with the physical condition of church properties are most severe for churches with membership of fewer than fifty or more than one thousand. It may be that these congregations are more beset by declining resources or increasing members, but it is also true that these extremes on the membership spectrum are most vulnerable to pride. The small congregation's property was good enough for their ancestors, and they are not about to change it now (certainly not to make room for parking). The large congregation has been successful in growing membership until now, and they aren't about to adopt a different tactic.

Unfortunately, in asking about space needs, the F.A.C.T. study has missed the point. Denominational studies usually miss the same point. The point is that it is not about *facility* anymore, but about *technology*. Therefore, the research discovery that congregations often need more education and fellowship space only identifies that neither churches nor researchers have awakened to twenty-first-century challenges. Vital churches are far less pressured for education and fellowship space, because the cell group and the Internet have transformed culture. The question to ask is "How many and what kinds of churches are taking advantage of contemporary technology and small-group tactics to pursue ministries of education and fellowship?"

The paradox in the F.A.C.T. study is this: On the one hand, congregations that are high on denominational heritage are likely to be in good financial health. On the other hand, congregations that are open to change are likely to be in good financial health. Yet congregations with a strong loyalty to heritage are probably less likely to be open to radical change. The answer may lie in the fact that strong denominationally loyal churches are more successful in tapping denominational subsidies, or more successful in attracting bequests from aging denominational loyalists; or it may lie in the fact that entrepreneurs who welcome change are more adept at raising money to do it. However, the F.A.C.T. study may provide an additional answer in revealing that churches with high credibility as moral beacons in the community, and congregations with high expectations for the behavior of their members, are generally in better financial health. The charitable dollars are out there. The public gives money to those organizations they most respect. What is alarming about chronic operating deficits, therefore, is not that people are poor, but that church and church leaders may not be credible to the general public.

This connection between financial health and credibility is a point missed by both meandering dilettantes and lost crusaders. The former assume that the public will respect their heritage, and give money for the sake of the heritage. The latter assume the public will admire their cause, and give money for the sake of the cause. Both are disappointed, and tend to blame the public for being too trendy or indifferent. Both fail to realize that the public will give generously to credible leaders with a large compelling vision. The blame lies with the churches and not the public. If the leaders are not credible, and if the vision is not broad and compelling, the people will not give.

## Leadership and Conflict Resolution

The F.A.C.T. study confirms that clarity of purpose and membership expectations dramatically reduce the potential for serious conflict, and when such conflict does occur, the same clarity helps resolve it. In other words, clear explicit consensus over core values, beliefs, vision, and mission is more important in order to resist or resolve conflict than are bureaucratic accountability procedures. This sounds quite reasonable, but it is disturbing how often churches miss the point.

The study reinforces habitual misapprehensions about vision. It suggests that cloudy vision has to do with congregational age and community context. Older congregations have less clarity of vision than younger ones, and rural or town churches have less vision than churches in new suburbs. However, the fact that suburban churches have younger people, more resources, or more programs does *not* mean that they have clearer vision. They are just as likely to be meandering dilettantes or lost crusaders as anybody else. It's just that their resources are positively fueled by the demographic flow of people and money to urban/suburban areas.

The strength of the F.A.C.T. study is that it confirms a very alarming truth about congregational dependencies on professional, certified clergy.

> But the fact remains that . . . congregations with leaders who have a seminary education are . . . far more likely to report that . . . they perceive less clarity of purpose; more and different kinds of conflict; less person-to-person communication; less confidence in the future and more threat from changes in worship. (p. 67)

The shock of this statement is not quite conveyed by the rather bland recommendation of the report that "these findings would suggest the need for a careful review of the educational process for leadership preparation" (F.A.C.T. study, p. 67). These findings reveal the need for a veritable revolution in the way churches grow leaders!

The real problem is not that congregations are too old or under-resourced to have a clearly motivating vision, but that they have leaders who are not energized by a vision. The F.A.C.T. study reveals that the higher the pastor's level of education, the less clear the congregation is about its purpose. (The study also reveals, by the way, that the better educated the clergy, the less likely the congregation will be to use the electric guitar in worship.) However, the study has only revealed one-half of the codependency that is shattering the fragile harmony of church life. The less committed the laity are to serious faith formation and outreach, the less vital and visionary the congregation becomes. Educate the clergy, and obscure the vision; educate the laity, and sharpen the vision.

## The Bottom Line

Whatever the strengths or weaknesses of sociological studies about churches, the conclusions are more disturbing than reassuring. This is the "reality" test that sociological research needs to temper the naïveté of measuring the opinions church leaders have of themselves.

- The vast majority of churches are not nearly as "vital" and "alive" as church insiders would like to believe.
- Over half the churches in North America are declining by any measuring stick you choose, and the ones that are growing are too often dependent on the temporary beneficial flow of positive demographics than any clear mission.
- Social service ministries are not having the impact on communities that they once had, and the growing dependency on nonprofit, parachurch, and govern-

ment help is distorting the truly traditional purpose of the church to multiple disciples.

- The increased cooperation of religious institutions is more a sign of a shared *lack* of vision, than of a shared vision.

The sociological studies themselves reveal alarming truths about the declining vitality and mission of the body of Christ.

- Congregations may claim commitment to undertake outreach ministries, but use excuses about space, parking, and money to cover up the real cause of their inability to do so: They lack the desire. If they really want to do it, the tactics, money, and volunteer infrastructure can be found.
- Most congregations have low expectations for adult spiritual growth and personal lifestyle, and this is the primary reason the congregation loses vitality. This lack is directly connected to higher conflict about music and worship, and to increasingly chronic operating deficits.
- Resistance to congregational change has more to do with the fear of conflict than with actual conflict itself. Congregations are more fearful of losing a few sheep from the flock, than of forsaking the mission of Jesus to the world.
- The present dependency on seminary-educated leaders is now undermining the vitality and mission potential of the Christian congregation in North America.

I realize that sociologists may dispute various interpretations I have shared here, and that some may not share my mission bias to multiply disciples of Christ and turn them loose in the world. However, I believe most expert sociological researchers will confirm this bottom line.

## Pilgrim's Progress

There is an alternative to the church of the meandering dilettante or the lost crusader. It is a church of pilgrims. With due respect to

John Bunyan, however, my reference to "pilgrim's progress" has more to do with the core process of discipleship in the earliest church than the puritan ethic of westernized Christianity. It also has more to do with the healthier and ultimately more productive alternative to "crusade" in the Middle Ages. It is not just a spiritual journey, but also a holistic spiritual journey that is in constant conversation with colleagues and culture.

A pilgrimage is a journey undertaken for a holy purpose. The Gospels and Epistles are organized around such travels. Jesus travels around Galilee and Judea for the holy purpose of revealing both himself and his message as good news. Jesus even transforms the mundane trip home to Emmaus by a pair of disciples into a journey with spiritual import. The disciples are joined by a mysterious stranger who opens their minds to the scriptures. They "constrain" him to stay for dinner. He is revealed as Jesus in the breaking of bread, and disappears from sight. The obvious question is "Where did he go?" Presumably, he continued his journey to the destination that was his original purpose. "Where was Jesus going in the first place?" He was traveling on the road to Emmaus, the eternal journey to the gentiles. This "holy purpose" is the pilgrimage described in the rest of the New Testament.

The Acts of the Apostles unfolds as a series of road trips: Philip on the Gaza road with the Ethiopian official; Paul on the Damascus road encountering Christ; the apostles and evangelists taking ships to all parts of the Roman Empire to spread good news to the gentiles. Not only do these travelers journey with a holy purpose, but also they establish communities that pursue spiritual journeys with a holy purpose. There is a constant character of spiritual exploration and discovery, and of deepening faith, clarifying values, and daring witness that is central to Christian community. All this change and all this uncertainty is progress with a holy purpose. Christians are travelers, witnessing to an experience of grace, from Jerusalem to Judea to Samaria "and to the ends of the earth" (Acts 1:8).

The earliest church both intentionally and unintentionally abandoned "pilgrim's progress" to become "meandering dilettantes" or "lost crusaders." The more established the church became as an institution, the more this trend accelerated. Finally, the New Testament ends with the writer of Revelation uttering dire warnings toward "lukewarm" churches (meandering dilettantes) and "self-righteous" churches (lost crusaders). The more institutionalized the Christian movement became, and the more saturated it became with the assumptions of the education, media, and legal systems of the day, the more likely it was to abandon pilgrim's progress.

Everybody is on a journey. The pilgrim is on a journey with a holy purpose. It is not a form of spiritual tourism to revisit the sentimental roots of grandparent or explore the curiosities of other faiths. It is not a form of militant crusade to conquer ignorant or evil people to force them to adopt a particular dogmatic or ideological agenda. It is pilgrimage. The pilgrim may detour to discover and learn, but soon returns to the holy purpose. The pilgrim may aggressively confront robbers or right wrongs along the way, but returns consistently to the holy purpose. Chaucer's *Canterbury Tales* gives a humorous, but accurate description of pilgrimage. It can be merry, somber, innovative, traditional, and is a great leveler of class-consciousness. Above all, the pilgrim's progress is companionable as people travel on their holy purpose in good company. Above this, the pilgrim's progress accompanies Jesus, because his companionship is what, in fact, makes the journey holy. Jesus is traveling on the road to Emmaus (or Cleveland or Sydney or Taipei) for a holy purpose, and his companions are with him.

The holy purpose to make and multiply disciples of Jesus is the point of the church. Tactics vary, but the purpose remains the same. It implies change of faith, change of lifestyle, change of relationship, change of attitude, and change of expectation, change of life itself. It would be a mistake to associate this great purpose with residence in any one location or embodiment in any specific cultural form. Discipleship will be expressed in infinite nuances, and the church in Ephesus will undoubtedly and legitimately behave differently from the church in Rome or Athens or Alexandria or Cleveland. The purpose is not to protect a heritage, or create harmonious fellowship, or win victories for sociopolitical causes, but to make and multiply disciples of Jesus. That may imply appreciation for certain aspects of the past, it may lead to harmonious fellowship, and it may cause social change, but the point of the pilgrimage is none of this. The point is to make and multiply disciples. (See figure 3F.)

Ancient Christians assumed that the pagan public was hostile to their faith, and alienated from relationship to Christ. Centuries

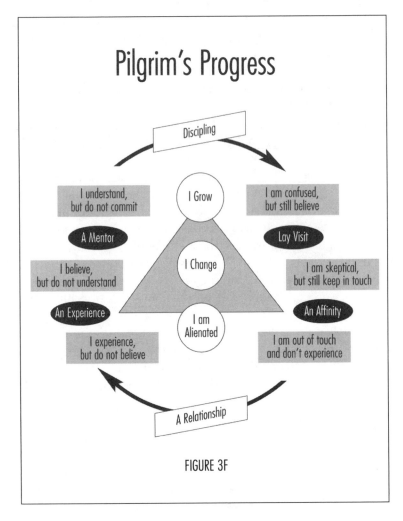

# Pilgrim's Progress

Discipling

I understand, but do not commit

A Mentor

I believe, but do not understand

An Experience

I experience, but do not believe

I Grow

I Change

I am Alienated

I am confused, but still believe

Lay Visit

I am skeptical, but still keep in touch

An Affinity

I am out of touch and don't experience

A Relationship

FIGURE 3F

later this alienation would be described as "original sin." It was not incidental sin. It was not that they were merely ignorant of the faith and needed to be better informed. It was not that they were blind to the cause, and needed to be enlightened. Even if they wanted to "know," their faculty of knowing was critically impaired. Even if they were convinced of the cause, they were not able to choose it. Ancient church people understood that the public was hostile to them, because unless they experience grace they could not be anything else.

Therefore, offer them an experience of grace. An explanation will not do and a symbolic act of consciousness-raising will not work. In worship, in relationship, or in chaos they need to be touched by the Holy. Once the Holy has intervened in their lives (worshiped in Athens as "the Unknown God" and recognized by alcoholics as "the Higher Power"), one should then help people understand who and what has happened. In order to do this, do not put them in a classroom or a boot camp, but offer them a mentor who can speak from his or her own pilgrimage experience of Jesus, fully human and fully God, the mysterious paradox that is so crucial to abundant life. The pilgrim's eventual commitment is not a pledge to participate in a stewardship process, or an enlistment to further a cause, but a covenant of discipleship. Discipleship means altering an entire lifestyle in the model of Jesus, and submitting to the authority of Christ, along with accepting responsibility to discern how all of this is nuanced by one's own life context. Discipleship is absolute surrender to Christ's mission.

Even pilgrims experience adventures and tragedies along the way. When church people become confused by gratuitous evil or unexpected conflict, do not send the clergy to visit. Send a volunteer, a Christian layperson, or a companion in the pilgrimage who can speak from personal experiences of life struggle and spiritual victory. If people still wander from the pilgrimage, do not send them a book or give them a videotape. Help them bond with a small group of fellow travelers based on a shared enthusiasm or affinity. If they leave the pilgrimage entirely, offer them a personal relationship that invites them back into an experience of grace.

No doubt some people will still wander from the church, but they will be few. In the pilgrim's progress of vital churches, they will not shed the church like a cocoon or resent the ecclesiastical overhead. There will not be much overhead left (the earliest church had little property to maintain and few personnel salaries), and deepening covenant of discipleship will continue to reveal new challenges and mysteries. People will also be less likely to accuse the church of hypocrisy or complain of being betrayed. Shared spiritual growth breeds humility and reduces unrealistic expectations. Deeper covenant relationships provide higher personal support. In the end, there are two kinds of people who leave the pilgrimage:

1. They are people who don't want to be pilgrims anymore. They do not enjoy holistic personal growth. They no longer want to surrender their lives to a holy purpose. They would rather stop along the way, open an alehouse, vacation in Florida, and otherwise entertain themselves. Let them go. They may become pilgrims again, but the longer you linger in the alehouse or their Florida condominium awaiting their change of heart, the farther behind your church becomes in walking with Jesus into mission.

2. They are people who want the pilgrimage to be changed into either a stewardship process or crusade for a cause. They want to impose boundaries between the sacred and secular, and impose their ideological and dogmatic convictions on other people. They want to hunker down in an institution, or charge off in limited direction. Heed them not. They may become pilgrims again, but if you surrender the integrity of the pilgrimage you will lose your way. You may catch sightings of Jesus from a distance, but you will no longer be walking the identical road.

The people who leave the pilgrimage will be those who are obsessed with control. They want to control their own destiny, rather than surrender to Holy purpose. They want to control other people, rather than celebrate a covenanted companionship.

Modern people assume that the holy purpose of pilgrimage is to travel to a particular location. How they get there, how much time it takes, who they talk to along the way, what side trips they enjoy, what ideas and skills they learn, what accidents and adventures befall them, or what trials they endure are all irrelevant. Modern people fail to understand that the holy purpose of pilgrimage involves not just a destination, but all of these other things as well.

Pilgrimage is a true alternative for the meandering dilettante because it shifts attention from tactics to mission itself. It refocuses spiritual life away from curiosities, and church membership away from trivialities, to concentrate on the whole point of living. Pilgrimage is a true alternative to militant crusade because it shifts the emphasis from confrontation to conversation. Pilgrimage organizes the enormous diversity of life around the unifying thread of discipleship.

## Why Is It So Hard to Renew Churches?

One of the most frequent comments I hear from denominational leaders and independent consultants is that it is easier to plant a new church than to renew an established church. Why is this? Every sociological study on congregations confirms that resources in money, property, technology, organizational infrastructure, and leadership are either present or obtainable. Even the poorest church in North America has more resources than an average church elsewhere in the "two-thirds world." The Billy Graham Evangelistic Association and many other evangelistic groups have been claiming countless Christian conversions for decades. Federal and regional governments in North America all prefer to have vital religious communities as a source of community cohesion and social service. Christians are constantly praying for the life and well-being of the church. So why is it so hard to renew a North American church?

Fundamentally, churches cannot be renewed until they have clarified their mission focus. This is not news. Congregations everywhere have spent many months, long hours in meetings, and untold staff and lay energies developing mission statements. Most of these mission statements are refined and crafted to the last iota and jot, celebrated with great fanfare, printed on worship bulletins or marketing handouts, and even carved in wood on the wall of the narthex—and then immediately forgotten. Nothing changes. The problem is that these mission statements have very little to do with mission.

- Meandering dilettantes actually do not want mission focus. They prefer a strategic plan. These plans resemble the itinerary of a busload of tourists who all have different places they want to visit. They negotiate the destinations, the routes, and the timing of the trip so that as many individual tastes can be satisfied. The wonderful thing about strategic plans is that they can always be adjusted by an ad hoc committee, and by the time five years have passed, most people have forgotten the itinerary anyway.

  The mission statement of meandering dilettantes is usually a pithy summary of the mandates of all the committees currently in place. Organizationally speaking, it is not a summary of where they are going, but simply a statement of how they are constructed. The actual destination remains foggy and probably unobtainable ("peace on earth," "the just society," "universal love," etc.). Meandering dilettantes love to speak of journeys, but are very unclear about destinations. The journey is simply the chronological passage of time, not a pilgrimage with a holy purpose.

- Lost crusaders do not really want mission focus either. They prefer dominant aggressive leaders. Political lobbying ensures that their individual or faction chairs the agenda, budget, personnel, and trustees committees. These leaders resemble an army's elite officer corps.

The wonderful thing about dependency on aggressive leaders is that one can follow them without really caring about the destination, and if a leader becomes too demanding, that person can always be assassinated (his or her *character*, of course!) or voted out of office.

The mission statement of lost crusaders is usually a pithy summary of the ideological or dogmatic cause of the organization. It is very clear about what the organization *is not*, and rather foggy and idealistic about what the organization actually *is*. ("We are not dogmatic, judgmental, exclusive, authoritarian, etc.") Lost crusaders love to boast about their pastors, lay leaders, and other community VIPs who attend the church, and enjoy name-dropping by citing the causes, non-profits, and prophetic people symbolic to their cause. They, too, speak of journeys, but more as a way of legitimizing the righteousness of their quest than celebrating the holy purpose of the trip.

The reason it is so hard to renew an established church is that members of established churches are unwilling to do the intense, partnered, constant adult spiritual growth that alone will clarify true mission.

Even in a church that yearns for pilgrim's progress, the presence of spiritual dilettantes and lost crusaders makes it extremely difficult for transformational leaders to multiply teams that lead change. If leaders rely on a phased, strategic, step-by-step transformational process, they are apt to feed the strategic-planning obsession of the meandering dilettantes, and the lost crusaders will attack the leadership as politically incorrect or dogmatically impure. If leaders rely on major staffing changes, and the appointment of aggressive leaders, they are apt to feed the obsession with hierarchy and faction of the lost crusaders, and the meandering dilettantes will accuse them of dictatorial control.

The only solution is for transformational leaders to redefine and clarify faithfulness by linking congregational life and mission to the original ancestors of the earliest church. With the help of consultants or mutual support networks of other transformational leaders, they begin to discern leverage points that can clarify purpose and redirect the energy of the church to the pilgrim's progress. My colleague, Bill Easum, and I have described these leverage points in various ways. The caution behind all of this, however, is that it is nearly impossible to leverage change in any congregational mix of dilettantes, crusaders, and pilgrims without losing some people. This directly contradicts the cult of harmony that lies at the heart of so many modern, supposedly traditional churches.

The final reason it is so hard to renew an established church is the most difficult to bear. There are fewer and fewer transformational leaders! A recent article in my city newspaper carried the headline: "Protestants Join Roman Catholics in Clergy Shortage" (*Guelph Mercury,* Saturday, August 25, 2001). Canada has now joined Europe in experiencing chronic clergy shortage as one more sign of steepening decline. The Bishop of the Evangelical Lutheran Church in Canada predicts that 20 to 30 percent of their congregations will be without a pastor in the near future. Seminary enrollments and denominational deployment have become increasingly dependent on second-career baby boomers for over a decade, just as churches have become dependent on the bequests of the builder generation to overcome financial crises. The reliance on bequests for financial stability, and the reliance on second-career clergy for church leadership are both short-term tactics rapidly running out of effectiveness. Even committed Christians are not choosing to be ordained and commissioned.

The article blames the clergy shortage on candidates "opting for more lucrative careers." Yet this is surely a misrepresentation. Coincidentally, there was another article from the associated Press in the same newspaper issue describing an eighty-year-old retired Baptist minister who had built an entrepreneurial mission to eastern Europe printing low-cost Bibles. He accepts no salary, and lives on his meager Social Security benefits. Similarly, there are many committed Christian disciples prepared to lead churches into real mission. They would be willing to work for smaller salaries, in challenging demographic contexts, but they are *not* willing to waste their lives playing chaplain to aging meandering dilettantes or diverting their energies to serve the political and dogmatic agendas of lost crusaders. The transformational leaders are there, but the modern traditional church does not really want them, and they don't want to be tied down to those churches. They would rather be with Jesus on the road to Emmaus to mission.

This brings us back to the most painful finding of the sociological studies of congregational life. The current pool of clergy trained by seminaries for professional ministries do not themselves have clarity of purpose. The F.A.C.T. study (p. 67) revealed that seminary-trained clergy are:

- less likely to serve congregations with clear purpose;
- less able to mentor potential leaders person-to-person;
- less confident about the future;
- more threatened than anybody else by changes in worship.

The work of church renewal involves inevitable conflict, and the F.A.C.T. study revealed that traditionally trained clergy are the least able to be in congregations that deal openly with conflict.

The lack of an ancient Christian mission for contemporary pagan times, and the lack of courageous leadership willing to disrupt the cult of harmony to pursue it, lie at the heart of the established congregation's inability to renew itself. Yet in the first chapter of this book I argued that it is possible for established church leaders to change. Like Peter, they too can experience a *Quo Vadis Moment.* How they build *Quo Vadis Momentum* to rescue the traditional organization and focus the confused missionary is the fragile hope to which we now turn.

## Four

## QUO VADIS *MOMENTUM*

The fragile hope of Christian mission in North America is that leaders will build on their own *Quo Vadis Moments* to generate in their congregations the *Quo Vadis Momentum*.

In the first chapter of this book, I identified the three basic categories of congregational participation. Identification by age, gender, marriage status, family structure, race, income, length of membership, office-holding authority, and ordination are irrelevant. The congregation today is divided among the following groups:

- *The Restless Ones:* They are convinced there are higher callings, bigger visions, and better ways to be the church. They may not know what these are, but they want to start looking for the answers tomorrow.
- *The Controllers:* They want the church to prop up their lifestyles and service their personal interests. They want the power to tell people what to think, how to behave, and what to do.
- *The In-Betweens:* They are relatively healthy, morally responsible, contented, generous people who are more concerned with membership privileges than mission.

The dynamics among these three groups shape congregational life and determine congregational mission.

*The Restless Ones* represent about 20 percent of the congregation, but are usually poorly networked. Their visibility depends on the emergence of poignant mission challenges that capture their imagination. They are more likely to negotiate with Controllers than motivate the In-Betweens, because the former always seems a faster track to get mission results. However, at heart they are self-starting entrepreneurs, and become easily frustrated with bureaucracy and hierarchy. They are radically generous to church outsiders, and perceive membership privileges to be mission restrictions.

*The Controllers* also represent about 20 percent of the congregation (although declining churches magnetically attract more and more controllers). They are highly visible through office-holding, choir presentation, and financial contribution, but are primarily networked through supper clubs, women's groups, or other social functions. They resist consensus about core values, beliefs, vision, and mission, so that they can impose aesthetic tastes, political perspectives, and personal prejudices as the boundaries for congregational creativity. They manipulate the Restless Ones by permitting occasional daring mission, and manipulate the In-Betweens by promising stability and harmony.

*The In-Betweens* represent about 60 percent of the congregation. Their visibility depends on the Christian year (more present on high holy days), their lifestyle cycles (more present with young children, marriageable youth, and aging parents), and their self-interest (more present in moderately bad weather, transitional recreation seasons, and ill health). The Restless Ones can motivate them provided that harmony is preserved, and the Controllers can manipulate them provided that their lifestyles are not judged. Once one convinces this group that relationships can be exponentially richer and self-fulfillment dramatically deeper by pursuing a greater vision, they will break old habits and renounce old hierarchies with reckless abandon.

*Quo Vadis Momentum* is generally a matter of networking and focusing the Restless Ones around an inclusive experience with

Jesus and a big vision of mission. Bypass negotiation with the Controllers as much as possible, and focus on motivating and mentoring the In-Betweens. Deliberately disharmonize the church by leveraging change with whatever tactic seems most contextually opportune. Demonstrate how personal fulfillment and profound relationships can be experienced in a deeper unity of purpose that lies beyond mere institutional habit.

There will be a period of significant stress as the Controllers realize their grip on congregational life is slipping. Their personal perspectives will no longer be the boundaries for creativity, and their power will no longer dictate mission. The degree of stress will escalate, and while leaders can use various techniques to explain, calm, and motivate, ultimately they survive by the authenticity of their Christocentric spirituality and the audacity of their inclusive mission. There will be a turning point, sometimes associated with a particular crisis and sometimes experienced as a general change of congregational climate, in which the congregation breaks free to a deeper serenity and confidence.

Thereafter, it will become easier to multiply mission teams to connect with all the microcultures of the community. This will eventually force the church to completely and formally reorganize the structures of the church, abandoning once and for all bureaucracy and hierarchy in favor of streamlined, team-based, empowering management.

The In-Between 60 percent of the congregation will ask, "Why should we change?" Leaders can and should offer a metaphor, image, or picture of a larger purpose and mission. However, recognize that what the 60 percent In-Between are _really_ asking is not "Why should we change?" but rather "Do we have to lose anybody?" The answer is a clear and inevitable "yes." People are going to leave your church in the next months and years. No matter what you do, no matter how you try, no matter how diligently the pastor visits, no matter how sensitive the middle judicatory becomes, no matter how much money you raise, no matter how many youth and children's ministries you deploy, no matter how beloved your pastor might be, you will lose people.

If the congregation does not change, the Restless Ones will leave. They will become impatient with the Controllers and frustrated by complacency meant to protect membership privileges. Indeed, many of these Restless Ones are leaving already. Their patience is now a fraction of what it once was.

On the other hand, if the congregation does change, the Controllers will leave. They will not be able to tell people what to do and how to behave. The institution will no longer shape itself around their personal or family needs. Indeed, many Controllers are already leaving simply because the resources of the church institution are now so diminished that there is little left to control.

Most of the In-Betweens will stay no matter what happens. Some may shift their involvement close to the center of church life, and others may shift their involvement to the edges, but so long as the church continues to offer them options to address their personal or family needs and worship preferences they will remain. They will be willing to surrender a degree of harmony if they are confident that by so doing they will form new and deeper relationships. They will be willing to risk more creative mission led by microcultures they do not really understand, provided they trust the integrity and vision of the core leadership.

Do not avoid the question "Do we have to lose anybody?" Address it head on, but refocus it on God's larger mission. The In-Betweens are coachable and teachable. Show them that they are *already* losing potential newcomers from beyond the church who go unnoticed by the Controllers, but who are among the best friends, neighbors, and work associates of the Restless Ones. These are the spiritually hungry, institutionally alienated people who look into the church briefly, and move on. They never joined the membership in the first place, so they cannot be easily tracked, but they have driven by, inquired among friends, experienced a wedding or baptism, tasted a worship service, attended a dinner, conversed as a stranger with some church member, and never come back. They represent most of the public, including the children and parents of church members.

It would be wonderful if you could motivate the In-Betweens simply with the words of Jesus to Peter: "Simon son of John, do you love me more than these?" (John 21:15). Do you love Christ more than fish and loaves, pews and liturgies, property and privilege? That motivation may come. The truth, however, is that you do not need to ask that question to motivate *Quo Vadis Momentum*. All you need to ask is: "Do you love controllers more than your own children, parents, neighbors, and work associates?" Is it more important to keep controlling clergy, matriarchs, patriarchs, wealthy trustees, or domineering institutional managers, rather than welcome your own teenagers, parents, and immediate loved ones into the community of faith? The choice may be as profound as "Christ or Institution," but for most people it is as simple as "Controller or my teenager." If one must go so the other can belong, what will be your preference?

In the first chapter, I used the metaphor of climbing a cliff face. The issue is momentum. You are clinging to a rope that you started climbing a short or long time ago. The climate has changed. The rope is icy and brittle; the wind is increasingly biting and strong. You might go up, and you may well fall down, but the one thing you will not be able to do for much longer is stay where you are.

## The Critical Path

The diagram on page 131 represents the critical path to building *Quo Vadis Momentum* for the church. It might be better to describe it as a "map" for spiritual leaders. This is not a linear, incremental step process. It is more chaotic than that. Spiritual leaders can initiate *Quo Vadis Momentum* at any number of points, and contextual circumstances might lead them in any number of directions, but the map describes the territory they must eventually cover.

For example, spiritual leaders might begin building momentum for mission by engaging a particular microculture, developing a program that affects that target public, and opens new doors for church growth. Increasing stress will force leaders to define their integrity and purposefulness through christological reflection and identity discernment. This will force strategic changes in leadership development and organizational structure. But it may well not happen like this for everyone.

So, for example, spiritual leaders might alternatively build momentum by casting a powerful vision and defining the core values, beliefs, and mission of the church. Then they might mentor a handful of disciples, who in turn will design and implement some creative ministry that will eventually transform the very core process of congregational life. Along the way leaders and laypeople will discover the importance of emphasizing adult spiritual growth, and begin to discover postmodern methodologies to do it.

Although *Quo Vadis Momentum* can be created in a variety of ways, certain principles seem to hold true among all spiritual leaders and in all cultural contexts.

- *Quo Vadis Momentum* rarely begins with organizational change. Constitutional restructuring, staff redeployment, or denominational polity change almost never precipitate much mission movement.
- Christology is always the center or pivot of *Quo Vadis Momentum*. It is the "binitarian" theology I discussed in my previous book, *Road Runner* (Nashville: Abingdon, 2002), and the answer to the key question: "What is it about our experience with Jesus that this community cannot live without"?[1]
- Leadership development is more important than strategic planning in developing and accelerating *Quo Vadis Momentum*. There is a nonlinear, both/and dynamic in which "growing people up" and "sending people out" are combined. The "action-reflection," "experiment-and-learn-from-mistakes" methodology holds true for both individuals and the body of Christ.

Perhaps the most important principle to keep in mind is that stress tends to emerge in three phases, each of which is related to the struggle between the Restless Ones and the Controllers in any given congregation. *Quo Vadis Momentum* will have to be sustained through three key barriers:

1. control of the spiritual growth methodology;
2. control of boundaries for creativity;
3. control of organizational permission.

These inevitable phases of stress may last for short or long times, they may involve sharp conflicts or chronic malaise, and they may be revisited at different points in the journey.

The best way to explain the critical path of *Quo Vadis Momentum,* and the phases of control that one will encounter along the way, is to describe the general movement of mission. Bear in mind, however, that this is not a blueprint for change in every situation, because every context will adjust the flow to its circumstances.

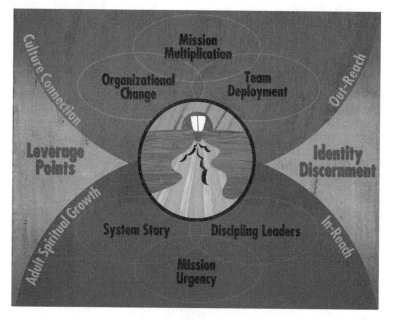

FIGURE 4A

## *The First Phase*

*Quo Vadis Momentum* begins when one or more spiritual leaders experience the *Quo Vadis Moment.* I have described this in the first chapter of this book, and again in *Road Runner.* It is the mission urgency to walk with Jesus into mission to the "gentiles." It is the passionate desire to leave the securities of Jerusalem to take mission to all the microcultures of the community. This desire is not primarily motivated by a philanthropic love of those microcultures, but by a desire to personally unite with Christ. As Paul says in Philippians (I paraphrase), "I consider all the securities and membership privileges I once had as so much rubbish, because of the surpassing value of knowing Christ, experiencing his sufferings, and sharing in his resurrection" (from Phil. 3:7, 8, 10).

It is difficult to prescribe how this "moment" comes about. If we understand Peter's experience on the rooftop to be normative from ancient times, then this moment comes about through a relationship with Christ, a period of intense brooding and experimentation, and conversation with people or microcultures outside your everyday experience. When the moment comes, it is usually in apocalyptic power. In other words, it leaves a person "thunderstruck" (amazed and excited), but also "changed" in the sense that their behavior patterns have been radically and permanently altered. In just such a way, Peter experiences the pouring out of the spirit on Roman Cornelius and his gentile companions and he is not only amazed ("Can anyone withhold the water for baptizing these people . . . ?" Acts 10:45, 47), but he is also changed. He no longer behaves in a manner that strictly adheres to the dietary laws and exclusivity of the Judaism of his time.

From mission urgency, the *Quo Vadis Momentum* is maintained by going in one of two directions. In actual experience, both directions are undertaken simultaneously.

First, momentum is maintained by discipling leaders. These disciples are handpicked, not nominated or elected, and they do not represent anyone other than themselves. They are chosen specifically for their *restlessness*, and not their *authority*, and for their openness to serious personal and spiritual growth. The *Quo*

*Vadis Moment* is passed on to them. The passion or desire to be with Jesus is awakened, along with the sensitivity to microcultures outside their usual experience. This mentoring process requires a significant investment of time and energy on the part of the spiritual leader(s) with whom *Quo Vadis Momentum* has begun. Mentoring is usually a combination of teaching and modeling, and one can easily imagine that it happens in the context of daily living more effectively than in meetings held in a church basement or parsonage living room.

Second, momentum is maintained by changing the model of core process or "system story" for congregational life. I have long maintained that the fundamental difference between a declining church and a thriving church is a matter of core process (system) rather than denominational polity (program). The core process, or flow of life experience, in *Quo Vadis Momentum* is that every day, in every way, as many people as possible are being *changed, gifted, called, equipped* and *sent*. In other words, people from all microcultures are experiencing God in ways that change their lives and lifestyles; discovering and receiving spiritual gifts that provide them a meaning and wholeness in life they have never known before; and discerning callings, which if pursued, will fulfill their life destinies. They are then equipped for the highest possible quality of excellence to pursue that great purpose, and deployed in teams of mutual support and continuous learning to do mission unencumbered by organizational bureaucracy. This core process contrasts sharply with traditional church experience. I compare this to the experience of the Jerusalem church in Acts, in which people were *enrolled, informed, nominated, supervised,* and *kept.* The earliest practice of the church was not to be in outreach to the gentiles, but to enroll people *into* the institution, inform them of all the correct information they needed to know, nominate them into management to implement the institutional agenda, supervise them lest they do inappropriate things, and ultimately, as a reward for dutiful service, preserve their membership privileges.[2]

While it is true to say that the "mental model" of leaders is being changed at this stage in *Quo Vadis Momentum,* it is insufficient to describe what is really happening. Core disciples are being trained in a certain pattern of behavior that they begin modeling for everyone else in the church. It is a never-ending circle of life experience. Once they are in mission and interacting with the public, they begin to ask questions about themselves, God, and one another they have never asked before. And the cycle of being changed, gifted, called, equipped, and sent starts all over again. This cycle is incomprehensible outside of the *Quo Vadis Moment,* and cannot be introduced to a church merely by adjusting program and policy. It is a habit that is ingrained in core disciples, and then modeled for others to follow.

Once the dynamic of mission urgency, discipling leaders, and core process is established, a broad ferment for adult spiritual growth unfolds. This is a form of in-reach in the sense that adults begin to go deeper, leap farther, and "be stiller" than ever before. To the outside observer, not much has changed in the life of the congregation. Yet to the inside participant, everything seems to be changing in the life of the congregation. Leaders (clergy and lay) have reprioritized time and are doing previously unexpected things. Expectations on the clergy for visitation and instruction are not being met in the same way, or with the same labor intensity, as leaders spend more time coaching personal and spiritual growth. Expectations on the membership for stewardship and office holding are not being addressed in the same way or intensity, and gaps are emerging in the institutional agenda, while at the same time members are being asked to engage in personal and spiritual growth.

It is here that the first phase of control emerges. *Quo Vadis Momentum* has empowered the Restless Ones, and has energized at least some portion of the In-Betweens. However, Controllers do not want to grow and do not want anyone else to grow. That is why they limit continuing education budgets and obsessively hire professionals to do as many ministries as possible. Personal and spiritual growth imply change, and change leads to instability, and instability inhibits the Controller's goal to shape congregational life around his or her personal agenda.

- Controllers do not personally want to grow. There is no motivation to do so. They make excuses about "busy lifestyles." While they value skills development in their own workplaces, so that their businesses can be more competitive, they do not value it for the church because they do not want the church to appeal to any microculture in which they may not exercise influence.
- More significantly, Controllers do not want anyone else to grow. In their opinion, sermons should motivate members to dutifully attend meetings, support the operating budget, and value internal harmony. If the members *grow*, they might imagine new things and behave in new ways.

The stress over motivation is usually experienced in the context of gaps in the institutional agenda. The focus on adult spiritual growth, for example, leaves a gap in youth or children's ministries. The emphasis on preaching to motivate spiritual growth has resulted in an operating deficit. The time spent mentoring chosen, restless people has resulted in nominations vacancies. The Controller's response is to focus controversy around these issues by rallying the In-betweens to hire a youth minister, sidetracking energy into a fund-raising campaign, or invoking judicatory intervention to shore up the bureaucracy. *Quo Vadis Momentum* demands higher continuing education budgets, patience or endurance with gaps in institutional organization, and a degree of financial risk not only on the part of the congregation regarding maintenance, but also on the part of the staff regarding salaries and benefits.

The subtler, but more powerful, exercise of control has less to do with motivation and more to do with methodology. After all, the Restless Ones have managed to inspire many In-Betweens to engage in serious personal and spiritual growth. Controllers may not be able to change that, but they can try to limit the methodologies with which people grow. They do this by insisting that learning methods be exclusively

- classroom contained;
- curriculum based;
- contextually neutral;
- technologically undersupported;
- relationally isolated;
- denominationally approved.

In short, this means that adult spiritual growth must take place in traditional classroom or church parlor settings using presentational and passive "schoolhouse" methods that even public education has abandoned. It must use a primarily print curriculum, articulating principles that are transferable without alteration to any culture or context, and which exercise only that part of the brain that is rational and abstract. Therefore, the learning program will not need to be enhanced by any sound- or image-based technology. It will depend solely on teacher/student communication (thereby increasing the need to hire professionals), and isolate the student from his or her peers, sending individuals home to study, not to the coffee shop to engage in dialogue. Finally, the methodology must use only those resources and teachers that are certified, published, or otherwise approved by the denomination.

In order to accelerate *Quo Vadis Momentum,* spiritual leaders must broaden the methodological options. They do not want to take away the above methodology completely, because for many In-Betweens that methodology might still work to take them deeper into themselves, their relationships, and their God. Instead, leaders need to multiply possibilities.

Methodologies should be:

- *lifestyle oriented.* Adult spiritual growth needs to be integrated into daily routine. This means it may be located away from the church building, and involve shorter or more flexible time periods. The additional suggestions below are all intended to make spiritual growth a pattern of living, rather than an intrusion on daily life. Premodern monastic models are actually good models for postmodern living, in that they seamlessly unite prayer, labor, learning, and leisure as a sacred experience.

- *talisman based.* Adult spiritual growth is motivated, anchored, and guided through images and sound bites, as it was in preliterate societies. In medieval times, for example, spirituality was guided by "devotional objects" depicting stories from Scripture or the lives of the saints that individuals found pivotal to their self-understanding. Intricately carved, golf-ball-sized prayer beads might open to reveal the three ages of man, a death mask, the four evangelists, the vanity of life, or tableaus of the Annunciation, nativity, Sermon on the Mount, Crucifixion, or Resurrection. Popular songs with spiritual lyrics and rhythms adjusted to work and walking were common. Such objects provided a focus for meditation, and an instructive reminder to recall the details of religious stories.

- *crucially contextual.* Adult spiritual growth is deepened when images and sound bites are adapted to the demographic and lifestyle context of the individual. Unlike curricula, talismans cannot be transferred from one person to another without modification. Nuances are just as valuable for spiritual growth and generic meaning.

- *technologically enhanced.* Technology is more than a tool that is essentially neutral to the meaning it conveys, but is itself part of the meaning. In my previous book, *Coaching Change* (Nashville: Abingdon, 2000), I devote an entire chapter to its significance in obstructing or empowering adult spiritual growth. In order to encourage spiritual growth by integrating it with lifestyle, adults must be able to pursue their uniquely designed pattern of growth through the technologies that they use every day.

- *relationally designed.* The mentoring relationship and mutual support network are more important than professional teaching. In part, this is because relational learning is more adaptable to diverse lifestyles. But also, since the learning is done in a peer group, relational learning helps nuance Christian truth for unique cultural contexts. Primarily, relational learning is important because the real point of the learning exercise is "growth," not merely "truth." The point of growth is not that people know what is correct, but that they shape lifestyle around what is good.

- *tied to congregational identity.* A spiritual growth path may or may not be approved by a denomination (and fewer and fewer people care), but it must be clearly tied to the core values, bedrock beliefs, motivating vision, and key mission that form the consensus identity of any particular Christian community. This is what binds the many individual and relational growth experiences to a larger whole that can inform, and be informed by, regular corporate worship. In such an environment, a common lectionary developed by religious experts is replaced by a common lectionary developed within the congregation by spiritual leaders.

It should be obvious that this track of adult spiritual growth will indeed liberate and motivate spiritual growth among the Restless Ones and the In-Betweens, but it will anger Controllers. The spiritual learning cannot be predicted in advance, monitored by experts, and controlled for institutional purposes. Since traditional learning methodologies are also offered, it becomes increasingly clear that the Controllers' warnings about losing "integrity" or "faithfulness" are really red herrings. The real issue is that Controllers cannot control the personal and spiritual growth of others, and mission breaks free from the limitations of institutional agenda.

In this first phase of *Quo Vadis Momentum,* denomination and seminary may either become tools for control or resources for spiritual growth.

The Controllers will try to manipulate denomination and seminary to block both the motivation and methodology of adult spiritual growth. In order to block motivation, Controllers will seek to unite with judicatories and academic centers to promote the myth that only certified, ordained professionals should guide adult spiritual growth. In order to block methodology, Controllers will pretend to worry about issues of truth and integrity, hoping to encourage the myth that only a hierarchy of appointed leaders with impeccable academic credentials can really articulate the truth. The churches will only provide continuing education funds for clergy, and clergy should only pursue continuing education through authorized academic centers or denominational programs. Congregational Controllers and judicatory or academic leaders all have their own reasons to inflexibly link spiritual growth and professional development. The seminaries need the income and wish to protect prestige; the judicatory enforces liturgical and political uniformity primarily through controlling personnel and pension; and the congregational Controllers can more easily control church life and program if they can manipulate staff.

However, this convergence of self-interest around the training, deployment, and control of professional personnel does not have to be. Denomination and seminary can resist this manipulation. They can do so from a larger motivation to multiply gifted, called, and equipped disciples of all kinds, who in turn will multiply Christian missions that will change local and global contexts. In the long run, it is advantageous for the denomination and seminary to abandon the link between spiritual growth and professional development. The ferment of amateur mission and lay spirituality is the original fire behind the Reformation in all its forms, and the growth of the ancient church itself. Seminaries have already discovered that greater openness to continuing education for laypeople and postmodern methodologies for spiritual growth will eventually enhance their relevance to the Christian movement, even if it limits their relevance to the Christian institution.

## The Second Phase

Once a cadre of core spiritual leaders has emerged who can imagine and model a different core process to respond to the urgency of mission, and who can motivate and model personal and spiritual growth for both the Restless Ones and the In-Betweens, and once a critical mass of adults begin to seriously engage in disciplined, partnered, spiritual growth, the congregation is ready to continue *Quo Vadis Momentum.* This will be done in three ways. These are not linear steps, but three simultaneous extensions of spiritual growth, the timetable for which will vary depending on congregational and community context.

The first path is *christological reflection,* or in other words, specific and wholehearted congregational focus on the significance of the life, death, resurrection, and ongoing mission of Jesus Christ. The Chalcedon Confession is the simplest and most direct expression of this focus: Jesus, fully human and fully divine, irrational paradox of incarnation, that is crucial for abundant life. Some congregations might explicitly use the writings of the earliest church leaders to help them focus on the significance of Christ, because for the first centuries of Christian experience the only question was "Who is Jesus and why should he matter to my microculture?"

It is important to understand that this christological reflection is not motivated by an academic quest to uncover the historical facts of Jesus, but by a desire to discern the existential import of the experience of Christ. This is why I repeatedly say that the key to church transformation is the corporate congregational answer to the question "What is it about our experience with Jesus that this community cannot live without?" Just as the goal of adult spiritual growth in the first phase of the *Quo Vadis Moment* is growth and the reshaping of lifestyle, rather than abstract truth, so also the goal of christological reflection is not "facts," but the experience of personal transformation and future hope. In other words, the point of this reflection is the same as it was for the earliest Christians: apocalyptic change.

A second path is *leveraged change.* Congregational leaders choose a particular tactic or program for which the opportunity is greatest and the stress is least, and devote prioritized energy to that tactic. The tactic might be an alternative worship service, capital campaign, property renovation, technology upgrade, a mission initiative, or any other program. In my book *Coaching Change* (Nashville: Abingdon, 2000), I identify the four most potent (and most stressful) leverage points: mentoring core leaders or board members, upgrading technology, new initiatives for adult leadership development, and worship. However, in my book *Facing Reality* (Nashville: Abingdon, 2001), I identify eleven different subsystems of congregational life, any one of which could contain a leverage point.

The selection of the leverage point is not arbitrary, nor does it simply depend on the resources of the church or the inclinations of church leaders. The selection of the leverage point is based on two criteria.

1. *A leverage point is chosen for the express purpose of disharmonizing the church.* Most traditional congregations have oriented themselves around a cult of harmony, and it is the stranglehold of this cult that must be broken for *Quo Vadis Momentum.* The leverage point is intended to raise stress levels among both Controllers and In-Betweens. Certainly one does not want to raise the stress level so high as to fracture the church irreparably, but stress levels should be high enough to force some people to consider leaving the church. Along with choosing the leverage point, multiply communications, offer opportunities for feedback, and reassure participants that leaders really are listening to learn from mistakes and refine the mission. However, most churches err on the side of complacency. They never raise the stress level enough to break the stranglehold of the cult of harmony. The real point of leveraged change is not merely to succeed with some strategy, but to use that strategy to disharmonize the

congregation and push people to a new level of cross-cultural sensitivity and mission awareness.

2. *A leverage point is chosen for the dual purpose of both beneficial outreach and growth in congregational participation.* The cult of harmony has rendered the congregation to be a homogeneous community that does not reflect the demographic and lifestyle diversity of the surrounding community. A good leverage point is one that not only blesses some microculture beyond the church, but which also draws that microculture to connect in multiple ways with the life of the congregation. Like the initial suction of a siphon, that one microculture in turn draws in other microcultures into congregational life. Not only does the congregation become more sensitive to other microcultures and macrocultures beyond the church, but also those cultures actually participate in the congregational experience. There is an unabashed "selfishness" to leveraged change.

Obviously, leveraged change will significantly challenge a congregation's Controllers. I will talk more of this shortly. It is essential in this phase, however, to focus attention on coaching the In-Betweens and the Restless Ones, and not allow spiritual leaders to be wholly sidetracked into negotiations with Controllers.

A third path is *identity discernment.* This is the process of building clarity and consensus around core values, bedrock beliefs, motivating vision, and key mission that form the "genetic signature" of each unique organism of the body of Christ. I established this organic metaphor in *Growing Spiritual Redwoods* and developed it in detail in my book *Moving Off the Map* (Nashville: Abingdon, 1998). I described the future use of this identity discernment for organizational change in *Christian Chaos*, but that is not the focus of concern in this second phase of *Quo Vadis Momentum.* Congregations may build clarity and consensus by starting with the entire congregation, over an extended time (perhaps nine months), using large and small groups. Or, congregations may build clarity and consensus by starting with core leaders, in intensive and prayerful conversation, using mentoring and membership training strategies to broaden ownership for the genetic signature.

The development of clear consensus for congregational identity not only builds unity, but also provides clear boundaries for creativity that provide deeper integrity for even the most radical experiments. This helps provide accountability for the Restless Ones, who are prone to charge off in any and every direction, and it also provides reassurance for the In-Betweens, who are eager to have some sense of spiritual continuity amid chaos and across time. Some congregations understand the importance of this consensus from the very beginning, and can build consensus before ever attempting to leverage change. Most congregations, however, do not immediately understand the importance of such consensus because the cult of harmony lies hidden in their consciousness. Only when leveraged change occurs do people realize the necessity for the unity and boundaries of a genetic signature.

At some time during this phase, congregational stress will reach its peak. That stress may focus on a particular tactic or issue related to program or staff deployment, or it may be more diffused through all aspects of congregational life—even to the supper clubs and coffee hours. The Controllers will become increasingly alarmed. Their alarm comes from not only the creative initiatives that are happening beyond their direct supervision, but also from the fact that the fundamental orientation of congregational life, which revolves around their self-interest, is being changed. The essence of their control is that congregational programs and staff deployment should address their personal and family needs, and be limited only by their aesthetic taste, political perspectives, and heritage preferences. That inherent selfishness can often appear quite benevolent. In this phase spiritual leaders are pushing *Quo Vadis Momentum* beyond "permission giving" to the point that both permission giving and permission withholding become irrelevant to congregational life.

The common pattern of controlling behavior in this phase is to begin with "turf protection" in which Controllers try to demarcate their "fief" or define their "faction" apart from the rest of congregational life. Developing clarity and consensus among the Restless Ones and the In-Betweens undermine these attempts at dividing church program among a ruling elite. And this is precisely why Controllers will attempt to sabotage the consensus-building process. The more broadly based the identity discernment process is—involving more and more large and small groups, core participants, marginal members, dropouts, and the general public—the more readily this attempt to control can be defeated. (See *Moving Off the Map*.)

When failing to protect turf, Controllers will usually turn to parliamentary procedure and institutional dithering to stall leveraged change and identity discernment processes. Suddenly, Controllers who were previously critical of the denomination for imposing outside agendas on the church are now defenders of denominational polity and denominational heritage. They will develop one ad hoc committee after another, and send appeal after appeal to the judicatory. Intensive christological reflection combined with increasing cross-cultural sensitivity encourage a mission urgency and compassion among the Restless Ones and the In-Betweens that break the bureaucratic dam and free the energy of spiritual entrepreneurs.

When failing to stall *Quo Vadis Momentum* by polity and process, Controllers will usually turn to personal denigration and occasionally threaten spiritual leaders' lives, reputations, or family security. Anonymous death threats are not unusual, but slanderous accusations in congregation and community, abusive behavior in worship or fellowship, and attempts to curtail income, benefits, and career opportunities are more common. Much of this is done behind the backs of the In-Betweens, and relies on the cult of harmony to hush it up. Therefore, the more these actions become public knowledge, the more outraged and supportive the Restless Ones and the In-Betweens become. Leadership relies on coaching and support networks both within, and beyond, the local congregation.

When failing to force spiritual leaders to give up, lose their marriages, or experience emotional breakdowns, Controllers will ultimately "take hostages." They will threaten to leave the church and take their family, their offering envelopes, the choir, the youth group, or other beloved people with them. This is the ultimate threat for the cult of harmony, in which it is always more important to keep people than welcome people. The hostages that Controllers threaten to take with them are always the sacred cows of congregational life: children and youth, memorial objects and selected heritage, money and prestige. At this point, leaders lead by the authenticity of their spiritual lives and the audacity of their biblical vision.

This is the reason so much time and effort has been spent on adult spiritual growth, identity discernment, and christological reflection. The critical factor, and the last battle, will be fought neither on the experience of Agape, nor on the experience of Phileos, but on the intensity and shared enthusiasm for Eros. Controllers are very fond of talking about "sacrificial love," because they can use that ploy to make the In-Betweens feel guilty that their unwillingness to bow to the personal wishes of a few will force some veteran members to leave. Controllers are also very fond of talking about "fellowship love," because they can use that ploy to make the Restless Ones nervous that they might find themselves all alone. The critical factor, therefore, is not to talk about Agape or Phileos, but to concentrate on *desire*. Ultimately, *Quo Vadis Momentum* depends on the degree to which the Restless Ones and the In-Betweens really, really *want* to be with Jesus on the road to mission.

Controllers will try to manipulate denomination and seminary to block all three paths in this phase. They will want the judicatory to become rigid and legalistic about denominational polity. They will want the seminary to criticize the Christ focus that is experiential and apocalyptic, and sidetrack clergy and lay leaders into doctrinal formulas, historical analysis, or expert opinions. They will want the denomination and seminary to standardize a generic set of values, dogmas, and missions that are transferable to every congregational "franchise" regardless of context. In short, they will want denomination and seminary to behave in the corporate models that became so popular in the late nineteenth and twentieth centuries.

However, denomination and seminary do not have to behave in this way. Denominations can recapture the spirit of their earlier entrepreneurial ancestors from the days of Reformation or the days of frontier ministry. Most denominational polities carry within them a pragmatism and readiness to adapt that twentieth-century legalists have tried, and failed, to bury. Seminaries can recapture the mission to grow disciples of Christ and train Christians for mission, and not just try to educate theologians and equip spiritual dilettantes. *Quo Vadis Momentum* needs partnerships for mission, and not overseers of personnel. It needs coaching for lay leadership, and not merely for professional development. Denominations and seminaries do not have to be manipulated by Controllers, and they can become vital partners with the Restless Ones and coaches for the In-Betweens.

Ironically, once having made the decision to decisively turn away from the cult of harmony and pursue *Quo Vadis Momentum,* most of the Controllers stay. They move to the edges of official leadership, and they may even diminish their financial giving, but as long as the church provides them with options that can address their personal needs, the relationships they have with friends who are part of the Restless Ones or the In-Betweens will keep them within the congregation. A few will leave. Most will not. Those who stay will actually become healthier as time goes by, as their obsessions to control or be controlled are moderated by association with a larger biblical vision.

The congregation breaks through to serenity it has never known before. Peace at any price has been replaced by greater unity purposefulness. This serenity may follow the departure of a few angry people, or the resolution of a particular issue, but often it emerges as a different climate in congregational life. It is like a change in weather, as unstable low pressure is replaced by sunny skies. Leaders suddenly realize their stress level is lower and they do not need to take antacids before every meeting. Nothing is changed—the same operating deficit is there, the same worship liturgy is performed, the same opportunities and obstacles are in place—and yet everything has changed. A fresh spirit and a new attitude pervade congregational life.

## *The Third Phase*

Even though the congregation now experiences greater serenity and focus, *Quo Vadis Momentum* continues. Indeed, if conflict was the major threat to momentum in the past, complacency can be the major threat to momentum now. As we shall see, "control" will surface again in another guise.

Now that the congregation has greater clarity of identity, and new initiatives are drawing in people from beyond the former circle of congregational life, a kind of chaos both energizes and threatens to overwhelm congregational leaders. Mission urgency sensitizes the congregation to all the emerging microcultures of the community, but there are so many needs, so many methods, and so many options that leaders hardly know where to start. They begin with a comprehensive plan for ongoing "research."

- Regularly reviewing demographic and lifestyle trends;
- Deploying teams to listen to the public and engage microcultures in dialogue;
- Regularly conversing with other community partners compatible with their genetic signature;
- Combining local and global conversations to offer a "reality check" for their perceptions. Yet this research is not merely sociological. The congregation treats its own spirituality as a methodology to discern and equip mission;
- Maintaining significant biblical reflection by core leaders;
- Continually developing strategies for prayer and meditation among leaders and members;
- Reading historical material—often using original writings—from the first six centuries of the Christian Era;
- Intentionally designing worship options around "missional purposes" of healing, coaching, cherishing, and celebration.

The congregation makes "culture connection" an environment of constant learning and adaptation. This is not outreach in the sense of a stable, unchanging organization deploying programs that benefit others. This is outreach in the sense that respectful interaction with others is constantly reshaping the organization itself to improve its ability to connect the gospel with every emerging microculture.

There are two factors that prevent the congregation from simply exhausting itself in an explosion of outreach energy. Neither of these factors involves any restructuring of boards or any particular reorganization of the church. These are more profound changes in habitual thought and behavior.

First, the congregation uses its clear consensus about values, beliefs, vision, and mission as a vehicle of accountability. It habitually thinks in terms of "boundaries" instead of "tasks." Rather than overwhelm leaders and members with long lists of duties and obligations, it frees leaders and members for rapid and faithful action by defining boundaries beyond which any activity must not go. This is the emergence of what Bill Easum calls "permission-giving leadership." It is not that leaders exercise powers of management, but that they become the primary articulators of the genetic signature of the congregation. They identify and embody the core values, beliefs, vision, and mission of the church. These boundaries are so vividly clear within and beyond the church that everyone can see the limits of action for themselves. This new, habitual way of thinking becomes the source of integrity and foundation of trust that remains the one constant amid the chaos.

Second, the congregation uses its emphasis on adult spiritual growth as the birthing environment for all missions. It habitually behaves in processes of self-fulfillment rather than self-denial. Rather than overwhelm members with a duty to implement the agendas of every microculture of the community, it expects members to discern mission as it is elicited by the spirit from their personal growth. This is what I have described in *Christian Chaos* as "bottom-up" mission. It is mission that is the fulfillment of one's life that emerges from the sociological and spiritual "research" of culture connection. This prevents mission from being simply the brainstorm or pet project of influential persons in the congregation (clergy or lay), and grounds mission in a deeper sense of faithfulness and personal joy.

It is remarkable that in the chaos that initiates the third phase of *Quo Vadis Momentum,* people are able to sustain focus and energy. The genetic signature held high by the core leadership helps the whole congregation avoid confusion and frenzied futility. The high expectations for spiritual growth modeled by core leadership helps them avoid burnout. Nevertheless, unless *Quo Vadis Momentum* continues further, even the most permission-giving and spiritually growing congregation will eventually plateau in outreach.

In this phase of *Quo Vadis Momentum,* congregations reorganize the church and restructure the board because of the necessities of *mission,* and not because of the necessities of *denominational polity.* In order to rapidly deploy mission for unpredictable opportunities that are faithful to the gospel, and that have enduring impact for changing lives and changing society, the old organizational models with which congregations have been operating must change. I describe this change in some detail in *Christian Chaos.*

The fundamental building block of the new organization is the "true team." Unlike old style committees and task groups, the true team has real power to discern, design, implement, and evaluate mission without ever asking the permission of a board. True team members are trusted to be in such entrepreneurial partnerships because the genetic signature of the congregation is intentionally scribed on their hearts. These are the boundaries beyond which they cannot go, no matter how creative or innovative their work. They are empowered to be such spiritual entrepreneurs because every true team is also a partnership for spiritual growth that is anchored in regular worship.

This means that the key to culture connection and outreach is not program development, but leadership development. This is the fruit of the core process first identified in phase one of *Quo Vadis Momentum,* in which people are changed, gifted, called, equipped, and sent. Disciples are grown, ministers are trained, and servants are deployed. In *Coaching Change*, I describe in detail the mission urgency, work ethic, opportunism, and winning faith that is central to the leadership development process of the church. My point here is that *Quo Vadis Momentum* will only be sustained when clergy and administrative leaders of the church surrender control of the mission agenda, and allow authority to be diffused among a multiplying number of true teams. Leadership multiplication and the entrusting of mission to more and more gifted, called, and equipped laity, is the whole point of the core process.

The proliferation of true teams pushes the church to Organizational Change. This proliferation creates a "servant-empowering organization" similar to what I have described in *Christian Chaos*. A "Stability Triangle" of three management teams grows disciples, equips ministers, and uses the assets of the church to deploy servants. These teams coordinate, communicate, acquire and use assets, and seed emerging mission—within the boundaries of the congregation's genetic signature and specific executive limitations—but they do *not* approve or disapprove of projects, nor do they fully subsidize the emerging team missions with a unified budget. The congregation also reorganizes the board. The board delegates management to a trusted, gifted few who form the management teams, and frees itself to discern long-term mission, measure the real impact of personal and social change, and set the standards of expectation for personal and spiritual growth. Finally, the congregation relinquishes all management, trusting its leaders to lead with integrity, and intentionally and regularly defines, refines, and celebrates the genetic signature.

Perhaps one of the most dramatic transformations of organizational change is redefining roles and redeploying staff. Most of the tasks commonly associated with the clergy have now been handed off either to true teams or (in the case of highly specialized ministries requiring certifications from government or other agencies) entrusted to specialists. Even these job descriptions have been rewritten "proscriptively" as explained in *Christian Chaos*. Staff are equipped with a clear mission purpose, scribed with the genetic signature, provided with a handful of executive limitations, and turned loose. The clergy are not even doing the traditional ministries of word, sacrament, pastoral care, and service in the ways of old. What do the clergy do? They envision the future, motivate mission, model genetic code, and coach the emerging team leaders of the church.

Mission multiplication is the fruit of the mission urgency begun long ago in the first phase of _Quo Vadis Momentum._ In ancient times, Paul and Peter multiplied the mission through Lydia, Priscilla, Acquila, Onesimus, Luke, Timothy, Apollos, and many others. They, in turn, multiplied the mission through thousands of others. They all shared a similar genetic signature, concentrated on personal and spiritual growth, and traveled in teams. Every team simultaneously did evangelism and social service. They never did anything to benefit another human being without sharing their faith motivation for doing it. They never shared their faith without doing something to benefit another human being.

The multiplication of mission is opportunistic and spiritually motivated. That means that at any given time in the mission field there are both redundancies and gaps. There may be multiple teams working to accomplish similar things, and the streamlined organization of the church can seed their mission and help them keep out of one another's way. There may also be community needs and mission opportunities that are not met, because the spirit has not yet elicited that from the hearts of the congregation. In the end, however, more lives are changed, more disciples are grown, more needs are addressed, more people are fulfilled, and more positive change has happened in the world than the congregation ever imagined possible. Instead of being one thing to a few people, so that by limited means, they could keep the gospel in the family, they are now all things to all people, so that by all means, they can share the gospel with anyone who will receive it.

Even now, there are still three kinds of people in the church.

The Restless Ones have actually increased in number, because the whole core process of the church is designed to make people restless. They are always discovering more about themselves, their relationships, and God. They are always discerning another mission to fulfill their life destiny. They are always asking new and deeper questions about God, their relationships, and themselves, as they interact with the public in mission. However, the Restless Ones now have a sense of fulfillment or joy they did not previously experience.

The In-Betweens represent about the same proportion of the church. Although many of them have been drawn into the flow of being changed, gifted, called, equipped, and sent, their numbers have been replaced by incoming seekers who tentatively test the experience of congregational life. In-Betweens usually come looking for Controllers to tell them what to believe, how to behave, and what to do, and are struggling with the combined disappointment that there are no easy solutions and the excitement that there are partners to help them find their own solutions. Some of the former In-Betweens are still in-between. However, they now have a deeper sense of unity and a higher trust of leaders, and they are happy to be along for the ride.

The Controllers may now be fewer in number, but they are still there and emerge in unexpected ways. The faces may be different, and indeed, they may now include your own. *Quo Vadis Momentum* brings out the hidden Controller in all of us. We hunger not only to be told what to believe, how to behave, and what to do, especially in times of confusion and stress, but also we hanker to tell people what to believe, how to behave, and what to do, especially in times of confusion or stress. And if anything, *Quo Vadis Momentum* can *increase* our sense of confusion and stress.

It is very common for the clergy, and even for some of the former leaders from the original "disciples" from the first phase, to suddenly be revealed as "hidden Controllers."

- Some core leaders who have stood by the transformational process through all the former conflicts will ultimately turn away from servant-empowering models and want to restore the old hierarchy and bureaucracy. Only this time *they* will be the ones to tell people what to believe, how to behave, and what to do. Now that they have freed the church from the tyranny of people who love organ music, they can subject the church to the tyranny of people who love easy listening music!

- Some clergy who have led the movement to reach out to all microcultures suddenly balk at surrendering their privileged roles as ministers of word, sacrament, pastoral care, and service to entrust them to emerging spiritual leaders and teams. The personal charisma that made them the center of attention and the spearhead of revolution in the past becomes irrelevant in *Quo Vadis Momentum* as clergy recede from the public experience of mission and retire from frenetic activity to model deeper spirituality. It is hard for a crusader to return to the monastery!

- Some church members will take advantage of the chaos and the freedom for initiative and try to manipulate or abuse others to address their personal agendas or serve their personal needs. They will try to convert true teams into committees and task groups. They may even try to take advantage of weakness and abuse the human rights of vulnerable seekers who are now being drawn into the community of faith. The intimacy and passion of the church also provides temptation for self-interest and personal profit.

The same principles and strategies that leaders applied with others to build *Quo Vadis Momentum* now need to be applied to themselves. The christological reflection, the boundaries of identity discernment, the commitment to adult spiritual growth, and the surrender to mission urgency are as important now as before.

These new Controllers will try to manipulate denomination and seminary to block the development of true teams and organizational change, and to limit mission multiplication. Even the best-intentioned, most supportive leaders of old can see the hidden Controllers emerge from their hearts as the chaos of mission exceeds even their expectations.

The hidden Controller will:

- want to defer mission in order to do incremental strategic planning that integrates the generic denominational mission strategy. Not only will this force entrepreneurial teams to fit themselves into an institutional agenda, but will also make the means of conducting the mission obsolete since the world will change before the strategic plan can be finished. Repeated ad hoc committees can slow down mission deployment indefinitely.
- appeal to the seminary to reserve certain "sacred" tasks unto themselves, so that in order to lead worship, share sacraments, hold office, or represent the church one must consult with a key person, central office, or follow a nominations process. Not only will this slow down leadership development with credentialing requirements, but it will ensure that staff receive a deference unavailable to anyone else.
- insist that the emerging servant-empowering organizational model interface smoothly with denominational polity. At least, this will both delay organizational change and slow down the core process of the congregation. At most, this will postpone organizational change indefinitely until the denominational polity itself is changed and stop the core process of the congregation. Teams will rapidly revert to task groups, and accountability will revert to supervision.
- introduce limitations on mission based on aesthetic taste or ideological preferences shaped by peer groups among the denominational judicatory or seminary alumni that have not emerged through congregational consensus, and that are imposed on the congregation as "good worship," "correct social action," or "pure dogma." Ownership of the genetic signature reverts from the body of Christ to the officers of the church, and becomes vulnerable to the personnel policies and curriculum changes of denomination and seminary.

These efforts to control often take congregations by surprise, and even surprise the leaders themselves. Only in this last phase of *Quo Vadis Momentum* do leaders reach their own limits of audacity and discover that they, too, must let go of professional habits and personal needs that have unconsciously shaped their behavior all of their lives.

Denomination and seminary do not have to succumb to this manipulation, but it will be difficult to avoid. Judicatories can recognize the congregation as the primary mission unit of the church, and guide bottom-up mission through supporting adult spiritual growth. Seminaries can train leaders in nonhierarchical and nonbureaucratic team-based organizational models. Judicatory leaders can extend flexibility to congregations to interface emerging organizations with denominational polity. Both denomination and seminary can create networks for retraining and mutual support for clergy and lay church leaders. All this is possible, but it will be hard. Judicatories will ultimately have to recognize that the top-down imposition of prophetic or dogmatic mission agendas simply does not work in the post-Christendom world. Seminaries will ultimately have to relinquish the privileged place of being the sole trainers of church leadership. Congregations swept away by *Quo Vadis Momentum* will carry on with or without judicatory and seminary partnerships.

*Quo Vadis Momentum* presents the church in our time with the same stress and opportunity that it did in ancient times. Already congregations and congregational leaders are being recalled to the head office in Jerusalem, both metaphorically and literally, to be reprimanded for their maverick ways.

- Why aren't you circumcising new believers?
- Why aren't you instructing converts in the Jewish dietary laws?
- Why aren't you doing the traditional "churchy" things we taught you to do?
- Why aren't you enforcing the denominational polity?
- Why aren't you implementing the judicatory agenda?

- Why aren't you teaching people to appreciate "good worship"?

At stake is the career path and financial security of the clergy, and the prestige and property of the congregation. But *Quo Vadis Momentum* has carried these churches and church leaders away. They say: "I consider all those wonderful things to be so much rubbish, compared to the surpassing worth of knowing Christ, and walking with Christ into mission." One can only hope that today, as they did long ago, church leaders will keep silent for a change and listen to the new Barnabas and the new Paul tell of "all the signs and wonders that God [has] done through them among the Gentiles" (Acts 15:12).

## Notes

1. During the earliest centuries of the church, before the Constantinian councils defined Christian dogma, Christian leaders talked about "God" and "Christ." The "Spirit" was understood as "the spirit of Christ." The "binitarian thinking" of the earliest church emphasized mystical experience over rational dogma, relationship with Christ over critique of other religions, and mission with Jesus over membership in institutions. Christ consciousness became the pivot on which all life and lifestyle turned.

2. See my book *Kicking Habits* or Bill Easum's book *Unfreezing Moves* for a more complete summary of core process and system story.

Five

# IS THERE ANY HOPE?

So, is there hope? I raise the question, not because I think I am particularly clairvoyant, but because so many church people and church leaders have asked it of me over the past ten years of consulting and coaching and it seems only responsible of me to try to answer it. The question hangs in the air in every denominational office, seminary classroom, and congregational annual meeting. Lyle Schaller dragged the question out into the open in his book *Tattered Trust,* a courageous and honest effort for which he was both praised and criticized. The question is asked of me all the time now.

Sometimes the question is asked by beleaguered judicatory leaders who are quelling yet another congregational conflict, watching credibility for the institutional church among the public dwindle by yet another scandal, or amalgamating yet another cluster of declining rural, small-town, or urban churches. Occasionally the question is asked by animated judicatory leaders who have planted a new church or launched a new mission initiative and wonder if it will thrive or even just survive the next ten years.

Sometimes the question is asked by disillusioned seminary faculty or by even more disillusioned seminary students who wonder if anyone really cares about salvation history, profound theology, biblical literacy, and lasting social change, or if the church merely demands leadership for institutional survival, pastoral care, memorial funds, and youth groups. Occasionally the question is asked excitedly by teachers or students with an innovative idea or creative mission who wonder if it has any chance of support.

Most often the question is asked by congregational leaders. Some of them are weary, abused, cynical, receiving anonymous death threats, or eagerly anticipating their retirement. Others are still energized, positive, leading relatively healthy congregations, confident that their community is better because the church existed last week, although they see the trends of aging membership and clergy leadership, shortage of clergy and fewer volunteers, lower stewardship and greater competition for the charitable dollar, lifestyle temptations, and growing indifference to organized religion.

Is there hope? Really? The numbers of church members and leaders who have burned-out, dropped out, or opted out have been swelled by members of the public who have walked away, turned back, or never considered the church a serious option in life in the first place. When church leaders ask the question, we must realize that they are by no means all hoping for the same thing. "Is there hope?" might mean:

*Will my denomination survive?*
*Will my church remain open?*
*Will there be a center aisle for my daughter's wedding ceremony?*
*Will the traditional rituals continue?*
*Will the Word continue to be rightly preached?*
*Will clergy be guaranteed a salary and benefits?*
*Will laity continue to get quality pastoral care?*
*Will Christian values and beliefs still shape public policy?*
*Will Christian congregations still be important features on the cultural landscape?*
*Will Christ still be relevant?*

*Will denominational resources and financial subsidies still be available?*
*Will quality professional clergy still be "recruitable"?*
*Will spiritually alive people still be interested?*
*Will gender- and generational-based Christian programs still be viable?*
*Will I, my children, or my grandchildren still have a great, nearby church service to attend?*

The question about hope can assume any or all of these questions, and it can be further refined by the particular existential situation of any particular believer. The point is that these are not hypothetical questions. These are real questions about the very next decades of our lives, and they are being asked not only by the majority of congregations that are declining, but also by the minority of congregations that are stable, and even by the smaller minority of congregations that are growing. Many of us started out in ministry having graduated with a large seminary class, and then were accompanied by a large fellowship of leaders and churches, and were supported by powerful and resourceful denominations. Thirty years or so later, most of our seminary graduation class has opted for other careers, companion churches have been dramatically reduced by closure and amalgamation, and denominations can no longer provide enough support even for maintenance. While timelines will vary from region to region in North America, the aspirations that lie behind all of the above questions are in serious doubt.

The real question, and the most ancient question, that needs to be asked is: "Will disciples of Jesus Christ multiply?" This is the question Paul, Luke, Lydia, and Priscilla asked. This is the question that Peter struggled so hard to answer. To this question I reply without hesitation: "Yes. Absolutely. Without a shadow of a doubt. It is already unfolding. Disciples of Jesus Christ are multiplying and will continue to multiply in North America." They may use different tactics. They may organize community in different ways. They may worship and grow spiritually and accomplish mission using a variety of methodologies. Disciples of Jesus

Christ can and will multiply. Some of them will be in megachurches. Most of them will be in microchurches. A few of them will be in middle-sized churches. In the demographic growth and lifestyle diversity of the pagan world, they may be rarer, but they will be of enormous worth.

I am not simply trying to be optimistic. There are reasons why I am so hopeful. They are similar to the reasons that made Peter so confident about the future of the earliest church.

First, *the hope of the church lies with the "gentiles."*

Two dramatic moments figure prominently in Paul's ministry. First, Paul and Barnabas preached to the synagogue in Antioch. After experiencing enormous stress, "they shook the dust off their feet in protest—and went to Iconium" (Acts 13:51). Later, Paul, Silas, and Timothy try again to transform the religious establishment, once again experience incredible resistance, and once again shake "the dust from [their] clothes." Paul declares, "From now on I will go to the Gentiles." He leaves the synagogue and goes *next door* to the gentile home of Titius Justus (Acts 18:6, 7). It is notable that the second incident happens after the Council of Jerusalem has tried everything possible to reconcile the gentile and Jewish Christians (Acts 15).

This act of literally going "next door" is now being repeated over and over again. If the Controllers and the In-Betweens of traditional established churches simply refuse to listen, Christian leaders are sacrificing career, family security, and pension plan to pursue the mission to multiply disciples for Jesus Christ. They do not even have to move to Iconium! They just have to go "next door." The spiritually yearning, institutionally alienated members of the public are the "gentiles" of our times and the fast growing demographic in North America. The hope of the church lies with them. They may have no previous experience with church, Christian, or Christ, but they are the most open to personal transformation, relationship with Jesus, and the fulfillment of their destinies to be in mission with Christ.

These churches may be house churches, or microchurches, denominationally sponsored churches derided as mavericks by their own judicatories, or newly planted faith communities specifically aimed at people of no Christian background. They may have many obstacles to overcome, but even if they perish in one neighborhood they spring up again in another. They multiply like weeds. They are not flowers. They may not be pretty, smell good, blossom all at once when the denominational sun shines, or stand together in orderly rows, but they endure. Even if denominations withhold resources and fail to water them, and even if pagan society tries to root them out of their backyard, they keep multiplying.

Second, *the hope of the church lies with people of color and non-Western culture.*

The earliest gentile mission thrived in a time of mass migration. Never in history until today were individuals and whole populations so mobile. Scriptural references contrasting "Jews and Greeks" were not only making a point about religious exclusiveness, but were contrasting "one race and culture" over against "a multiplicity of races and cultures." They may have spoken Greek or Latin in the same way that immigrants adopt English as a second language. This explosive multiplication of people "not like us" was the opportunity seized by the earliest Christian missionaries.

In part, this is the power of immigration. Christian leaders of color and from non-Western European cultures are bringing their christological clarity and mission zeal to North America. Their churches are becoming the transforming agents in American society. They recognize a mission field when they see it. Moreover, their focus to adapt Christian worship and spiritual growth to first-, second-, and third-generation immigrants is changing the way we think about Christian development and conversation with culture. Asian, Hispanic, African, Caribbean, Pacific Rim, eastern European, and Middle Eastern immigration are not only creating opportunities for Christian witness, but are bringing *their own* Christian witnesses.

In part, this is also the power of lifestyle networks. A new psychographic generation emerges every two or three years. Just as the transportation and communication innovations of Roman times multiplied lifestyle options and religious choices, so also television, Internet, and global travel have multiplied the diversity of even the most remote communities in North America. Outports in Newfoundland are watching the news from Ohio, and loners in the Miami inner city and finding networks in Brazil. Communities are being shaped around music, recreation, and lifestyle. The sociological evidence seems to indicate that the more culturally diverse a community becomes, the more people withdraw from *organized* religion to avoid conflict with their neighbors, and the more people connect with *relational and transformational spirituality*. It is the essence of Christianity.

Third, *the hope of the church lies with courageous, networked leaders*.

Traditional, transformed leaders did indeed help the earliest church multiply disciples. Even James, the brother of Jesus, perhaps the best known "traditionalist" in the Jerusalem head office, helped empower the mission to the gentiles. At the decisive moment in Acts 15, he affirmed Peter's vision from the rooftop and discerned what was essential to the gospel. Apollos was a Jew from Alexandria who spoke enthusiastically about Jesus, although knowing only "the baptism of John" (Acts 18:24, 25). With a little coaching from Priscilla and Aquila, he became one of the great, undocumented missionaries of the church. Acts and the Epistles are filled with references to others who teamed with the apostles, and more than a few were transformed traditionalists.

The same hope is unfolding today. Although denominations are struggling, there are judicatory leaders who, like James, have affirmed Peter's vision from the rooftop of diversity, and, like James, have had the courage to at least get out of the way. They have demonstrated flexibility, creatively interfaced with maverick congregations, and sheltered spiritual entrepreneurs from the storms of protest. Congregational and judicatory leaders who knew only the renewal movement of the 1970s and 1980s have been coached by contemporary Priscillas to become transformational leaders of traditional churches.

I know that many congregational leaders, both frustrated and successful, will have read the preceding chapters and said to themselves: "I know that transformation of a traditional church is possible, but is it likely?"

The fragile organization of the church can change, but is it *likely* that declining congregations will surrender the cult of harmony? There is a way to shift congregational unity away from taste, appearance, and sensibility, toward a consensus around shared values, bedrock beliefs, biblical vision, and positive outreach, but is that likely to happen? Can denominations *truly* help congregations develop serious grievance procedures? Can seminaries *truly* break the codependency between parish clergy and needy laity? Are congregations, denominations, and seminaries *likely* to break out of the narrow confines of sacred space, sacred time, and sacred people? Is that a weak, moderate, or strong possibility?

The church as confused missionary can change, but is it *likely* that declining congregations will surrender ecclesiastical "sacred cows" for authentic "discipling processes"? There is a way to move a congregation of meandering dilettantes or lost crusaders into faithful pilgrim's progress, but is that likely to happen? Can denominations surrender top-down control of the mission agenda, and *truly* help congregations elicit mission from the hearts of spiritually growing adults? Can seminaries develop accreditation paths that *truly* grow visionary church leaders? Are congregations, denominations, and seminaries *likely* to break out of the narrow confines of ideologically and dogmatically shaped agendas, and unite evangelism and social action once again? Is that a weak, moderate, or strong possibility?

Assuming that church leaders do experience a *Quo Vadis Moment,* how likely is it that they will be able to build *Quo Vadis Momentum?* There are, after all, three boundaries of control through which they must break free. It would be helpful if the denominational judicatory and the seminary resisted manipulations by the Controllers in order to empower the Restless Ones and coach the In-Betweens, but is that likely to happen? Even if it does happen, the obstacles can be enormous. The longer a church is in decline, the more it magnetically attracts dysfunctional people with a need to control or a need to be controlled, and most congregations have been in decline for some time!

Yet despite all this cynicism, I have encountered all across North America, in all denominations and ecclesiastical networks, more and more clergy and laity who are prepared to stake everything in order to build *Quo Vadis Momentum.* That is the miracle that gives me the most hope. There are more and more clergy who are willing to stake the parsonage and the pension plan to be with Jesus on the road to mission. There are more and more laity—and not a few of them senior citizens—who are willing to stake the property and the heritage to be with Jesus on the road to mission. They are not weighing the probabilities of success. They are discerning that most fundamental goal that will make their lives worth living.

These courageous leaders are seeking one another out, and building networks for mutual mentoring and mutual support. They are crossing denominational boundaries, even traditional Protestant and Catholic boundaries, to find partners with a similar genetic signature. They are crossing old boundaries between liberal/mainstream and conservative/evangelical polarities to forge a new species of church. They are even crossing racial, ethnic, generational, national, and cultural boundaries for faithful outreach. Denominations and seminaries need not be excluded from these networks, but they are rapidly becoming irrelevant to these networks.

Fourth, *the hope of the church lies with Christ.*

Since this book has been based on Peter as a paradigm for transforming traditional churches, it is fitting to conclude with one more relevant ancient story for the contemporary world. Peter is on the beach in Galilee again some time after the resurrection. People in stress often return to old habits and routines. He is still pondering the Great Commission to literally take the gospel on the road to all nations, and summoning the courage to leave the head office in Jerusalem. Jesus appears and begins cooking breakfast for him on the beach (John 21:9-17). He asks Peter the same question three times.

"Simon, son of John, do you love me more than these?" *Do you love me more than harmony? Do you love me more than balanced budgets, beautiful property, and classical organ music? Do you love me more than sacred space, sacred time, and sacred people?*

Peter, and increasing numbers of clergy and laity, responds, "Yes, Lord."

"Simon son of John, do you love me?" *Do you love me more than control? Do you love me more than denominational polity? Do you love me more than seminary academic degrees? Do you love me more than your favorite ideology and dogma? Do you love me more than the institutional church and your local church heritage?*

Peter, and increasing numbers of clergy and laity, responds, "Yes, Lord."

*Simon son of John, do you really, really love me? Do you love me so much that you will go as deep as you can possibly imagine in personal and spiritual growth? Do you love me so much that you will forget about membership size and personal privilege, and satisfy yourself with mentoring just a handful of disciples? Do you love me so much that you will change anything, and do anything, in order to help every person get to know me? Do you love me so much that you will accompany me into mission with every microculture of the community, and reorganize your life and your church to do outreach, and only outreach, and nothing but outreach, so help you God?*

Peter, and increasing numbers of clergy and laity, responds, "Lord, you know everything; you know that I love you." Jesus nods approvingly, and says, *Good for you. Now follow me, and let's go feed the sheep.*

Peter came a long way to reach Rome, and to experience the *Quo Vadis Moment* in which he turned around to follow Christ into mission to the gentiles. His *Quo Vadis Momentum* had carried him beyond tradition, beyond institution, and even beyond tactics. It carried him beyond fellowship, beyond philanthropy, and beyond even the memory of a comfort zone. The hope of the church lies in *Quo Vadis <u>Momentous</u>*. It is that momentous, climactic, eternal instant when a church leader realizes that all that matters is knowing Christ. Neither the past nor the future is relevant. Neither the survival of a church nor the success of a church really matters. The companionship of Jesus on the road to mission is its own reward.